NEW HORIZONS IN CRIMINOLOGY

I0223082

A CRIMINOLOGY OF NARRATIVE FICTION

Rafe McGregor

BRISTOL
UNIVERSITY
PRESS

New Horizons in Criminology series

Series editor: **Andrew Millie**, Edge Hill University, UK

New Horizons in Criminology series provides concise, authoritative texts which reflect cutting-edge thought and theoretical development with an international scope. Written by leading authors in their fields, the series has become essential reading for all academics and students interested in where criminology is heading.

Forthcoming in the series:

Transnational Criminology
Trafficking and Global Criminal Markets
Simon Mackenzie, October 2020

Out now in the series:

Imaginative Criminology
Of Spaces Past, Present and Future
Maggie O'Neill and **Lizzie Seal**, July 2019

A Criminology of War?
Ross McGarry and **Sandra Walklate**, July 2019

A Criminology of Policing and Security Frontiers
Randy Lippert and **Kevin Walby**, February 2019

A Criminology of Moral Order
Hans Boutellier, January 2019

Climate Change Criminology
Rob White, October 2018

Find out more at
bristoluniversitypress.co.uk/new-horizons-in-criminology

First published in Great Britain in 2022 by

Bristol University Press
University of Bristol
1-9 Old Park Hill
Bristol
BS2 8BB
UK
t: +44 (0)117 954 5940
e: bup-info@bristol.ac.uk

Details of international sales and distribution partners are available at bristoluniversitypress.co.uk

British Library Cataloguing in Publication Data
A catalogue record for this book is available from the British Library

ISBN 978-1-5292-0805-4 hardcover
ISBN 978-1-5292-0806-1 paperback
ISBN 978-1-5292-0809-2 ePub
ISBN 978-1-5292-0808-5 ePdf

Cover design by Dave Worth
Cover image credit: Alamy A28B74

Contents

About the Author

Rafe McGregor is Senior Lecturer in Criminology at Edge Hill University, UK, where he specialises in critical criminology and philosophical aesthetics. He is the author of *Narrative Justice* (Rowman & Littlefield, 2018), *The Value of Literature* (Rowman & Littlefield, 2016), two novels, and over two hundred journal articles, review essays, and short stories.

Acknowledgements

I would like to thank Alana Barton for being an exemplary critical criminologist and for her friendship.

Earlier versions of three of the case studies appeared in a previously published paper: Criminological Fiction: What is it Good For? *Journal of Theoretical and Philosophical Criminology*, 12 (January 2020), 18–36. I am grateful to editor-in-chief David Polizzi for his support.

NEW HORIZONS IN CRIMINOLOGY

Series editor: Professor Andrew Millie, Department of Law and Criminology, Edge Hill University, UK

Preface

Stories are hugely important to our understanding and experience of crime, justice, and social harm. We may like to think of criminology as a science where the causes, our experiences and responses to crime can be measured with accuracy. There is a place for such statistical analyses; but criminology is also interested in things that cannot be measured, including the stories we tell and the narratives we construct to explain our experiences. Stories have had an important place in the history and development of criminology, from Clifford Shaw's (1930) *The Jack-Roller* through to contemporary growth in narrative criminology (e.g. Presser and Sandberg, 2015). In this new book Rafe McGregor draws on this rich heritage to take narrative criminology in a new direction by constructing a criminology of narrative fiction. Rafe highlights how narratives have been important for criminological data collection and analysis and for providing a framework of understanding, but attention has tended to be on narratives derived from real-world experiences. In this book the focus is fiction – particularly narratives in crime fiction in cinema but also in novels, television series, and graphic novels. It is argued that fictional narratives not only provide criminologists with useful material to aid teaching and learning, but are also sources of real and meaningful data. According to Rafe, these can be phenomenological by representing experiences, counterfactual by representing possible situations that do not exist, or mimetic by accurately representing reality.

The aim of the New Horizons in Criminology series is to provide high quality and authoritative texts which reflect cutting edge thought and theoretical development in criminology, have an international scope and are also accessible and concise. This new book fits this description well in arguing for fiction to be taken seriously. Rafe takes the reader with him as he unpacks a theory of the criminological value of fiction. Ideas are explained clearly and illustrated by detailed examples from a range of international settings. The examples also represent an array of cinematic (and other) traditions, from box office crowd pleasers such as *Beverly Hills Cop* (1984), through to popular TV such as *The Wire* (2002–8) or *Broadchurch* (2013–17), or graphic novels such as *The Sheriff of Baghdad* (2018). Rafe is also able to draw on his own experiences including as a former South African police officer.

In some ways this book complements another in the New Horizons series – *Imaginative Criminology* – where Lizzie Seal and Maggie O'Neill draw from real life and fiction to explore relationships between space, place, memory and ideas of 'transgression, exclusion, resistance and possibility' (2019: 1). Rafe's interest is more philosophical and he is equally at home writing about criminology and philosophy – especially aesthetic education. This new book develops ideas from Rafe's previous text on *Narrative Justice* (2018: 106) where the definition of narrative justice was that 'criminal inhumanity can be reduced by the cultivation of narrative sensibility'. It was a bold claim, but highlighted the potential benefits of engaging with people's stories. In this new text Rafe's argument is that fictional narratives also have value.

Narrative criminology is gaining wider attention becoming much more than a niche interest for a few dedicated academics. In this little book Rafe makes valuable insights and contributions to theory in this developing area. By highlighting the criminological value of fiction he also draws attention to something where many outside of criminology can contribute. Crime fiction is hugely popular, and by arguing that it can provide meaningful criminological data also recognises that we might need to engage with experts outside of criminology – be they experts in literary criticism, media and cultural studies, aesthetic education, or members of the public who are fans of crime cinema. This book represents a valuable contribution to narrative criminology, but also to criminology more generally. It will also be of interest to other academics and students who are interested in stories. This is a very thoughtful contribution and I recommend that it is read widely.

References

McGregor, R. (2018). *Narrative Justice*. London: Rowman and Littlefield International.

Seal, L. and O'Neill, M. (2019). *Imaginative Criminology: Of Spaces Past, Present and Future*. Bristol: Bristol University Press.

Shaw, C.R. (1930) *The Jack-Roller: A Delinquent Boy's Own Story*. Chicago, IL: University of Chicago Press.

Presser, L. and Sandberg, S. (eds) (2015) *Narrative Criminology: Understanding Stories of Crime*. New York: New York University Press.

Introduction: Narrative, Criminology, and Fiction

Introduction

Bronwen Hughes' *Stander* (2003) is a cinematic biography of
Andre Stander, a captain in the South African Police who achieved
international fame as a prolific bank robber from 1977 to 1984. The
problem with the work from a criminological point of view is not
that it misrepresents the character of Stander, but that it reveals the
limitations of the discipline as it is for the most part practised in the
English-speaking world. Although the film purports to be a biopic,
Hughes fictionalises her protagonist to the extent that he bears
little resemblance to the reality and the directorial sleight of hand
is compounded by Thomas Jane, who plays the part with charisma,
charm, and pathos. Stander's egoism, hubris, and psychopathic
personality traits such as sexual predation and animal abuse have been
replaced with a self-sacrificial concern for the victims of apartheid for
which there is no evidence (Moorcraft and Cohen 1984). As such, the
film provides an example of why most criminologists are sceptical about
the criminological value of fiction and of the obstacles that must be
negotiated if fiction is to be brought into the fold of the discipline. The
problem for criminology, however, is revealed in the courtroom scene.
Referring to the internal stability duties he has performed on behalf
of the apartheid regime, Stander states simply: 'I'm tried for robbing
banks, but I have killed unarmed people' (*Stander* 2003). The judge is
not interested in his confession and Hughes suggests that there can be
no private moral responsibility in a public administration without a
moral compass. From a legal perspective, the judge is correct: Stander's
actions during the Soweto uprising of 1976 were not criminal under
South African law, but his armed robberies were. If criminologists
want to be able to say something about the greater of the two crimes,
apartheid, then they must look beyond the narrow confines of the law.

Criminology is, as the name suggests, the academic discipline that
takes crime as its subject. The concept of crime is a complex one and
Sandra Walklate (2017) identifies six distinct understandings: legal,

moral, social, humanistic, social constructionist, and harm. In order to grapple with this diversity, six are usually reduced to two: legal and harm. On a legal understanding, crime is behaviour that is prohibited by the criminal law of a particular country at a particular time. This is both the most obvious and the least sophisticated understanding as it makes no attempt to account for why certain behaviours – for example, men having sex with men (regardless of whether they identify as homosexual) – are legal in some countries but not others and both legal and illegal in the same country over time. On a harm-based understanding of crime, crime is behaviour that harms either a person or a group of people. Crime understood in terms of harm can account for categories such as crimes against humanity and corporate crimes, but an exclusive focus on harm runs the risk of diversifying the subject matter of criminology to the point where it is lacking in coherence. The harms-based approach usually takes 'social harm' as its subject and is sometimes referred to as zemiology, which is often regarded as a subdiscipline within criminology (Hillyard, Pantazis, Tombs and Gordon 2004; Boukli and Kotzé 2018). My approach recognises the significance of both of these understandings of crime and focuses on their intersection, i.e. on crimes that are socially harmful.

I take the aim of the criminological project to be the reduction rather than prevention of crime or social harm. I prefer the former term to the latter as it provides criminologists at the theoretical level and criminal justice practitioners and social activists at the practical level with an achievable goal. As such, the criminological value of an entity – whether concrete or abstract and including approaches, frameworks, theories, models, methodologies, and methods – is simply its value in reducing crime or social harm. The reduction of crime or social harm is achieved by employing theoretical and empirical investigation and verification to direct or inform public policy and evidence-based practice (Matthews 2014). The chain of causation from criminology to crime or social harm reduction proceeds as follows: criminological inquiry identifies the cause or causes of a particular crime or social harm; the findings of the research are translated into a policy for one or more government or private agencies with the aim of reducing or removing the causal factor or factors; and the policy is put into practice resulting in the reduction of certain types of crime or social harm or of the commission of various crimes or social harms by certain categories of offender (Sutherland 1947; Garland 2001; Agnew 2011). The key factor that links criminological research to crime or social harm reduction is the explanation of the cause of the crime or social harm. In consequence, the criminological value of approaches, frameworks, theories, models, methodologies, and methods can be assessed in terms of their value in explaining the causes of crime or social harm. In this book, I argue that fictional narrative representations can do precisely this, explain the causes of crime and social harm.

My position on the criminological value of fiction is both counter-intuitive and, at the time of writing, highly unpopular (Ruggiero 2003; Frauley 2010). All the previous attempts to explore the value of fiction, literature, or film for criminology have been framed as part of the expansion of the criminological imagination: as fostering a creative yet rigorous intellectual crafting that explores the relationships between private and public, agency and structure, and empiricism and theory (Mills 1959; Williams 1984; Frauley 2010; Young 2011). My argument is that the criminological imagination does not exhaust the criminological value of fiction and that fiction can provide actual data that complements the data provided by traditional academic and documentary sources. A consequence of this argument, which will be unpalatable to some criminologists, is that in virtue of their value in explaining the causes of crime and social harm, fictional narrative representations can be employed to direct public policy and the practice of criminal justice professionals. There are two considerations that could – and should – make this claim appear less extravagant. The first is that I defend three specific criminological values of fiction – phenomenological, counterfactual, and mimetic – which are all concerned with the conveyance of particular types of knowledge by narratives. My thesis is thus limited in terms of the types of knowledge conveyed. Second, narrative methods have been employed to both collect and analyse data in the social sciences for just over a century and nonfiction narrative representations are widely regarded as having criminological value in explaining the causes of crime and social harm. I demonstrate that the distinction between fiction and nonfiction in narrative representation is necessarily vague and that the association of truth with nonfiction is naïve. Before distinguishing between these two types of narratives, however, I must delineate narrative representation itself.

Narrative vs non-narrative

Stories are representations and a representation is something that stands for something else, for example a flag standing for a country or a word on a page standing for an object in the world. Stories are also an unavoidable part of everyday life in the twenty-first century. They are so ubiquitous, instantiated in so many genres, by so many modes of representation, and across so many media channels that it is easier to begin by identifying representations that are not stories. These include lists and diaries (with which all readers will be familiar), annals and chronicles (to be discussed later), most poems (particularly when one considers recent and contemporary poetry), and most conversations (where one may set out to tell a story, but usually fails courtesy of interruption, digression, or both). This book is concerned with constructing a criminology from a particular category of story, those that are fictional. With this end in mind, it is important to start with an uncontroversial definition of stories, one that reaches the broadest base possible. In consequence, I employ research from two different disciplines, selected on the basis of providing the most sophisticated analyses of stories, storytelling, narrative form, and narrative representation. The disciplines are literary studies and philosophy and the traditions within those disciplines are literary theory and literary aesthetics respectively. Literary aesthetics provides the most accessible entry point.

Writing in the tradition of literary aesthetics, Peter Lamarque (2014: 1) begins with 'the intuitive notion of a story. What is that notion? Minimally, just this: the representation of two or more events, real or imaginary, from a point of view, with some degree of structure and connectedness.' Noël Carroll (2013) defines narrative as the recounting of an event or state of affairs through an interval of time. He (Carroll 2013: 122) moves on to prototypical narratives: 'most narratives involve at least two, but generally more, events and/or states of affairs which are related or arranged temporally and causally (where the causation in question may include mental states such as desires, intentions, and motives).' Carroll divides narratives into two broad categories, episodic and unified. Episodic narratives consist of smaller stories where causal linkage is weak and frequently achieved by means of a recurring protagonist. Unified narratives are those that have a smooth transition from beginning to middle to end and where the end 'secures the feeling of closure in an audience' (Carroll 2013: 123). Gregory Currie (2010) initiates his discussion of narrativity by noting that all representations are created rather than found and therefore the product of a process of intentional shaping. He (Currie 2010: 27) claims that narratives 'are distinguished from other representations by what they represent: sustained temporal–causal relations between particulars, especially agents'. Peter Goldie (2012: 2) provides the following definition:

> A narrative or story is something that can be told or narrated, or just thought through in narrative thinking.

It is more than just a bare annal or chronicle or list of a sequence of events, but a representation of those events which is shaped, organized, and coloured, presenting those events, and the people involved in them, from a certain perspective or perspectives, and thereby giving narrative structure − coherence, meaningfulness, and evaluative and emotional import − to what is related.

He differentiates stories from lists, annals, chronicles, and many − if not most − diaries. Of the four philosophers, Currie (2010) is the only one to distinguish a story from a narrative and my starting point is to take the two terms as synonymous.

Literary theorist Tzvetan Todorov (1971) draws on the work of the Russian formalists to differentiate *fabula*, real or imagined events, from *sjužet*, the way in which those events are presented. Gérard Genette (1972) uses *histoire* and *récit* to identify a similar distinction, where the latter term is also called *discourse*. Peter Brooks (1984) notes that the translation of *fabula*/*histoire* as 'story' and *sjužet*/*récit* as 'plot' (followed by Currie) has been subject to much criticism and it does indeed misrepresent the crucial distinction at stake. The dichotomy with which literary theorists are primarily concerned is between a real or imagined *sequence of events* and the *story* of those real or imagined events. This distinction is crucial because whichever characterisation of narrative one prefers, narratives are representations of events, not the events themselves. Representations of sequences of events are *selective*, as Hayden White (1980: 11) demonstrates in his translation of the *Annals of Saint Gall*:

709.   Hard winter. Duke Gottfried died.
710.   Hard year and deficient in crops.
711.
712.   Flood everywhere.
713.
714.   Pippin, Mayor of the Palace, died.

An annal is a historical representation that is little more than a list of events organised chronologically. In the example, many more events occurred in 709 than the two described and the representation of a sequence of events will necessarily exclude some − or, more likely, many − of the events that occurred. White (1987: 280) explains this point with regard to historical representation: 'if history consisted of all the human events that ever happened, it would make as little sense, be as little cognizable, as a nature conceived to consist of all of the natural events that ever happened.' This is true of all narrative representations, not just narrative histories.

Lamarque (2014), Currie (2010), Goldie (2012), and White (1980) are all in agreement that narrative representation is gradational rather than categorical, that narrativity admits of degrees. Paul Ricoeur (1980: 169) defines *narrativity* as 'the language structure that has temporality as its ultimate referent,' but this is both too restrictive and overly inclusive. There are some narrative representations of sequences of events that do not employ language and some linguistic representations of sequences of events that appear to lack the features typically associated with narratives. Narrative representations of real and imagined sequences of events can be communicated by a variety of means, including the written and spoken word and still and moving images. In the remainder of this section, I shall not distinguish between narratives that represent real and imagined events or between linguistic and visual (or descriptive and depictive) narratives. An uncontroversial definition of narrative representation at its most inclusive can be derived by synthesising research in literary aesthetics and literary theory to identify a *minimal narrative* as: the product of an agent that represents one or more agents and two or more events which are connected.

The manner in which the representation of agency and the representation of event contribute to narrativity is straightforward, but the connection among events has been subject to much debate. Lamarque (2014: 52) takes the broadest view of this requirement, claiming that:

> there must be some more or less loose, albeit non-logical, relation between the events. Crucially, there is a temporal dimension in narrative, not just in the sense that component sentences are tensed but also in that there must be a temporal relation between the events, even if just that of simultaneity.

Carroll (2001: 126), like Currie (2010), favours a stronger connection: 'the earlier events in the sequence are at least causally necessary conditions for the causation of later events and/or states of affairs (or are contributions thereto).' I shall accept the weaker, temporal connection between events for minimal narratives while acknowledging that non-minimal narratives have a causal connection between events and that 'exemplary narratives' (Currie 2010: 35) have a causal connection which is so strong as to contribute to the thematic unity of the narrative. Currie (2010: 39) defines thematic unity as follows: 'unity is provided by a focus on some common thread in the activity of particular persons in particular connected circumstances, though narratives often do have, in addition, general thematic unity in that we are invited to generalize from the case in question.' The importance of thematic unity restricts exemplary narratives to the type Carroll categorises as unified.

There is a further feature of narrativity that emerges from thematic unity, *closure*. White (1980) employs Richerus of Reims' tenth century *History of France* as an example of a chronicle, noting that the text has a central subject, geographical and social focus, a demarcated beginning, and a narrative voice. What is absent, however, is a conclusion and the representation merely terminates *in medias res*,[1] leaving the reader to connect the end of the sequence of events with its beginning. Within White's taxonomy of historical representations, it is this absence of closure that characterises the text as a chronicle rather than a narrative. White maintains that closure is linked to meaning, which can be shifted by narrative representation as form is imposed upon a sequence of events, creating layers of cognitive, emotional, and evaluative significance. In my terms, chronicles meet the criteria for minimal narratives, but the absence of closure precludes them from the category of exemplary narratives. My conception of closure as a criterion for the latter is general and Carroll (2013: 123) expands on the feeling of closure mentioned previously by describing it as 'the almost palpable sensation that the story has finished–up at exactly the right spot'.

Taking these advances on minimal narratives into consideration, an *exemplary narrative* can be defined as: the product of an agent that is high in narrativity in virtue of representing one or more agents and two or more events which are causally connected, thematically unified, and conclude. The most obvious differences between minimal narratives and exemplary narratives are thus the causal relations, thematic unity, and closure of exemplary narratives. These three features combine to create a perspective that is absent in minimal narratives. Exemplary narratives are essentially perspectival, a point Goldie (2012) makes clear by defining narrative structure as the presentation of a sequence of events and the people involved in them from a particular perspective. Lamarque (2014: 9) refers to this perspectival nature as opacity:

> narratives are "opaque" somewhat as paintings are opaque. They have the same kind of intentionality, not just as products of intentions, but also, in different ways and to different degrees, through expressing thoughts or a point

of view on what they represent. This seems to be true of all narratives, not just those of literary fiction.

The perspective that constitutes an exemplary narrative produces a *framework*, which Currie (2010: 86) identifies as 'a preferred set of cognitive, evaluative, and emotional responses to the story'. In other words, the creators of narratives invite those who experience them to adopt certain emotional responses and evaluative attitudes to the characters, actions, and settings represented. The opacity described by Lamarque provides an initial indication that narratives do not represent in a manner that can be considered transparent, objective, or neutral.

The following seven are all examples of exemplary narratives, meeting the five criteria established earlier and characterised by their opacity and an identifiable authorial or directorial framework: Francis Ford Coppola's live action film, *The Godfather* (1972); Derek Raymond's (1984) novel, *He Died with His Eyes Open*; Roméo Dallaire's (2003) memoir, *Shake Hands with the Devil: The Failure of Humanity in Rwanda*; Ari Folman's animated documentary, *Waltz with Bashir* (2008); USA Network's television series, *Queen of the South (season 1)* (2016); Ava DuVernay's live action documentary, *13th* (2016); and Megan Abbott and Alison Gaylin's (2018) graphic novel, *Normandy Gold*. With respect to philosophy, Currie (2010: 34) claims that it is not the concept 'narrative' that is philosophically interesting, but 'the concept *thing high in narrativity*'. This is also the case for criminology and from this point on I shall use the terms 'story', 'narrative', and 'narrative representation' to denote exemplary narratives unless otherwise specified.

Fiction vs nonfiction

As my list of seven exemplary narratives indicates, 'narrative' should not be conflated with 'fiction', although the terms are often used interchangeably – and with good reason, as I explain later. Dallaire's memoir, Folman's animated autobiography, and DuVernay's live action documentary are works of nonfiction that represent real people, places, and events in a manner such that the representation has an apparently substantial correspondence with the reality. There is nothing about these three works that makes them any lower in narrativity than the other four, but the difference between nonfiction and fiction seems to be significant. The idea that there is a correspondence between representation and reality in the former three that is absent in the latter four is a popular – probably the most popular – way of distinguishing nonfiction from fiction. 'Nonfiction' is a familiar term, which includes both the also-familiar 'documentary' and the less-familiar 'faction'. 'Faction' denotes one of two genres of representation, New Journalism and the nonfiction novel (Lamarque 2014). New Journalism is characterised by reporting that draws attention to the subjective experience of the author instead of aiming for objective description. Truman Capote's (1966) *In Cold Blood: A True Account of a Multiple Murder and Its Consequences* popularised the nonfiction novel, which is an ostensibly transparent representation of reality that employs the form and techniques of the (fictional) novel. Literary theorists in particular have been concerned with works that cross the boundary between nonfiction and fiction, like fictionalised biographies, and with applying literary theory to nonfiction, such as White (1980) on historical representation. My position is that the boundary is not only porous, but to at least some extent arbitrary.

The relationship between correspondence and nonfiction is usually conceptualised in one of three ways. On the first and most naïve, nonfictional representations are characteristically true and fictional representations characteristically false. The approach is not supported by either literary theory or literary aesthetics and runs into immediate problems due to 'false' being a pejorative term, denoting either accidental error or deliberate deception (Lamarque and Olsen 1994). To accuse Coppola of being in error in *The Godfather* because he tells a story about Michael Corleone (played by Al Pacino), a person that did not actually exist, is to the misunderstand the production and reception of fiction. The representation of Corleone could not be in error because there is no real person with which it could or should correspond and it is not deceptive because both Coppola and his audiences are well aware of its fictionality. A second way of approaching the distinction is to focus on the relationship between the representation and the readers or audiences that experience the representation. In this account, nonfictional representations invite audiences to believe their content and fictional representations invite audiences to make-believe or imagine their content (Walton 1990; Spivak 2012). I used this as a placeholder in the previous section when I referred to sequences of events being either real or imagined. The distinction is applied as follows: where DuVernay invites her audiences to believe that mass incarceration in the United States is a method of disenfranchising African American citizens in *13th*, Coppola invites his audiences to imagine that the Corleone family was part of the New York Mafia in *The Godfather*. The crucial flaw in this account has been exposed by Derek Matravers (2014), however, who points out that all thick representations – those that are vivid, rich, and gripping – require readers and audiences to employ their imagination in the experience of the representation. There is thus no essential difference between imagining the (actual) events in Rwanda described by Dallaire and the (fictional) events in London described by Raymond. The third approach distinguishes nonfiction and fiction by means of their content, which is (or was) existent in nonfiction and is invented in fiction. In this account, fictional representations are invented and, in consequence, provide more scope for authorial or directorial creativity (Belsey 2011; Attridge 2015). The distinction is insufficiently robust, however, as there is an important sense in which the content of *The Godfather* is existent and the content of *13th* invented.

Sarah Worth (2017: 45) provides an articulate description of the blurring of the boundary between existence and fiction:

> On the surface, fictional texts are ones that are considered "unreal." They did not happen. When we look deeper, however, it is not that simple. Part of what it means to understand or appreciate something as fictional is to be able to turn the fictional descriptions into conceptual mappings that we know how to make sense of. That is, although what happens in fiction did not *actually* happen, the events described in most fictional literature do happen in familiar kinds of places, with descriptions of plausible relationships; they are about familiar kinds of situations, and they involve recognizable motivations, feelings, and resolutions. We are able to make sense of fictional descriptions because they are often not so different from descriptions of real events, people, and places.

The relation between fictional people, places, and events in fictional representations and the world is often understood in terms of reference to universals (McGregor 2016). The notion is from Aristotle's (2004) famous observation on the superiority of poetry over history: history refers to what has happened (particulars) and poetry to the kinds of thing that can happen (universals). This is one of the meanings of the various conceptions of the idea of truth in or of fiction (Lewis 1978; Potter 1998; Gibson 2007). For example, although *The Godfather* does not represent the change of leadership in a real Mafia family, Michael Corleone's acceptance of his criminal inheritance is accurately described as true to life, lifelike, or resembling reality in virtue of representing the type of person that adopts such a role. This relation is not restricted to characters, settings, or action in the representation, but to the representation as a whole considered in terms of its theme. Despite representing fictional people, places, and events, USA Network's *Queen of the South (season 1)* is thus true to life, lifelike, or resembles reality in representing the close relationship between victimisation and offending in the experience of criminalised women.

The blurring of the boundary between existence and fiction is also evident in the opposite direction, between invention and nonfiction. In the previous section, I noted that the imposition of narrative form on a sequence of events creates layers of meaning within a representation – particularly (but not only) cognitive, emotional, and evaluative. This is part and parcel of the process by which exemplary narratives represent reality in an opaque rather than transparent manner and is a consequence of the selectivity essential to narrative representation. Narratives standardly ignore, omit, or condense those parts of the sequence of events that lack relevance to the central plot, thematic unity, or overall coherence of the representation. Once again, this notion extends back to Aristotle (2004), who praises Homer (2003) for his unity of plot in the *Odyssey*, where the sequence of events takes place over a decade. Selectivity and opacity are features of all exemplary narratives, whether fiction or nonfiction. In *Waltz with Bashir*, for example, Folman could not represent all of the relevant events between his service in the Israel Defense Forces in Lebanon in 1982 and the making of the film two decades later and his deliberate (and accidental) omissions alter the cognitive, emotional, and evaluative significance of the representation, which is necessarily opaque. The intentional shaping of an existent sequence of events into an exemplary narrative with an authorial or directorial framework represents those events from a particular perspective such that the framework undermines the categorical distinction between existent and invented narrative content. In other words, whenever an author or director decides to represent a sequence of events in narrative form, there is at least a sense in which those events are fictionalised.

If I am right and truth and invention can be found in both fictional and nonfictional narratives, is there any point in attempting to distinguish between them? Matravers (2014) and Worth (2017) think not and focus instead on the differences between thick and thin narratives and well-constructed and badly-constructed stories respectively. In *Narrative Justice* (McGregor 2018b), I was similarly dismissive of the distinction, arguing that both documentary and fictional exemplary narratives have a role in explaining the causes of ideologically-motivated crime and social harm. In this book, however, I am concerned with fictional representations, because they have been marginalised within criminology. In consequence, the distinction between fiction and nonfiction is significant – which is why this is a criminology of narrative fiction, that is a criminology of fictional exemplary narratives, rather than a criminology of narrative. The most promising way to make the distinction is by means of Peter Lamarque and Stein Haugom Olsen's (1994) conception of fiction as a rule-bound practice that informs a particular type of communication between an author or director on the one hand and a reader or audience on the other. To create a work of fiction in a verbal or visual tradition is to make a fictive utterance and to experience that work as a work of fiction is to adopt the fictive stance. The authorial or directorial invitation to experience a work as fiction is matched by a set of expectations in readers and audiences. The expectations associated with the practice of fiction differ from those associated with the practice of nonfiction. Typically, there is a desire for a closer correspondence between representation and reality in the practice of nonfiction and a greater tolerance for inventiveness, imaginativeness, and fabrication in the practice of fiction. In addition to avoiding the pitfalls of the true/false, belief/imagination, existent/invented dichotomies, the conception of fiction and nonfiction as different practices explains why the former practice has been – and continues to be – marginalised in criminology. Fiction as a practice involves the creation of works that are both produced and recognised as fictions and of which most criminologists are dismissive: there is little correspondence with reality and a great deal of fabrication, in consequence of which fictions have nothing to offer with respect to the reduction of crime or social harm.

I began this chapter by identifying the aim of the criminological project as the reduction of crime or social harm and the role of criminological research within this project as the explanation of the causes of crime or social harm. I then distinguished narrative representation from non-narrative representation. I differentiated between minimal narratives, which hold little interest for the criminologist, and the exemplary narratives with which I shall be concerned. I provided examples of the latter across different modes of representation (novels, graphic novels, films, and television series) and both fiction (*The Godfather, He Died with His Eyes Open, Queen of the South [season 1], Normandy Gold*) and nonfiction (*Shake Hands with the Devil, Waltz with Bashir, 13th*). I claimed that in all cases, exemplary narratives could be characterised by an opacity with respect to the sequence of events they represent and by an identifiable authorial or directorial framework on those events. I concluded by explaining some of the complexities of attempting to distinguish nonfiction from fiction in terms of truth, belief, or existence and adopted a conception of fiction as a practice in which representations are both produced and experienced as fictions. The significance I have accorded to exemplary narratives and to fiction as a practice provide the foundation for my development of narrative criminology in a new and perhaps not entirely welcome direction. In the final section of this chapter, I sketch this direction in a little more detail.

The structure of this book

The rest of this book constitutes an argument for a criminology of narrative fiction, that is for a theory of the criminological value of fiction. I begin with a critical analysis of current work in narrative criminology and current criminological work on fiction. I distinguish my theory from current criminological work on fiction and classify it as emergent from the narrative criminological framework. I then demonstrate the phenomenological, counterfactual, and mimetic values of narrative fiction. I conclude my argument by explaining the relationship between the aetiological and pedagogic values of narrative fiction,[2] focusing on cinematic fictions in virtue of the vast audiences they reach courtesy of their place in global popular culture.

Chapter 2 sets out six levels of criminological inquiry – approaches, frameworks, theories, models, methodologies, and methods – in relation to narrative representation. I identify the subdiscipline of narrative criminology, as pioneered by Lois Presser (2008, 2013, 2018), as a framework and characterise my theory as emergent from this framework. Although Presser is exclusively concerned with nonfiction narratives, we share a realist approach to research, a commitment to the view that stories can reduce social harm just by being stories (that is, irrespective of their truth value), and an interest in narrative form.

Chapter 3 situates my criminology of narrative fiction in relation to the contemporary criminological engagement with fiction. I distinguish my theory from three others: the various theories within the cultural criminological framework, the critical realist framework adopted by Vincenzo Ruggiero (2003) and Jon Frauley (2010), and my previous work within the narrative criminological framework (McGregor 2018b). My claim is that none of these engagements employ narrative fiction as a case study, as a source of criminological data.

Chapter 4 initiates my argument by demonstrating the phenomenological value of fiction, which is the value of the representation of the subjective experience of offenders. I present two case studies, Martin Amis' (2014) *The Zone of Interest* (a novel) and Tom King and Mitch Gerads' (2018) *The Sheriff of Babylon* (a graphic novel). In each example, the fictional representation conveys knowledge of what it is like to be the perpetrator of social harm (the National Socialist genocide in the former and the American occupation of Iraq in the latter) and, in consequence, provides an explanation of the cause of social harm.

Chapter 5 demonstrates the counterfactual value of fiction, which is the value of the representation of what psychologists call counterfactual thinking and philosophers call possible worlds. I present two case studies, ITV's *Broadchurch (series 3)* (2017) (a television series) and Marlon James' (2014) *A Brief History of Seven Killings* (a novel). In each example, the fictional representation conveys knowledge of counterfactuals – situations that have not happened but might, could, or would if circumstances differed – that provide insight into the causes of crime (in the former) and social harm (in the latter).

Chapter 6 demonstrates the mimetic value of fiction, which is the value of the capacity to provide knowledge of the world by representing everyday reality in detail and with accuracy. I present two case studies, both drawn from the cinematic mode of representation in consequence of its greater mimetic value when compared to other modes, Michael Mann's *Miami Vice* (2006) and Fernando Meirelles and Kátia Lund's *City of God* (2002). In each example, the fictional representation conveys knowledge about the everyday reality of organised crime that would be difficult (if not impossible) to convey in a documentary.

Chapter 7 examines the relationship between the aetiological (phenomenological, counterfactual, and mimetic) and pedagogic values of narrative fiction. I argue that these values are complementary by establishing the concept of criminological cinema, which recognises the potential of cinematic fictions to convey vast amounts of perceptual and other information to an audience of millions of people in a rapid and readily accessible manner. I use one of the two most-watched crime films to date, Martin Brest's *Beverly Hills Cop* (1984), as a case study, demonstrating the ways in which it facilitates, augments, and enhances the communication of knowledge of intersectionality.

Chapter 8 summarises the argument for a criminology of narrative fiction presented in the four previous chapters and explains why cinematic representations should be the focus of future inquiry into the criminological value of narrative fiction.

2

Narrative Criminologies

Introduction

The structural turn in literary criticism began with Russian formalism in the second decade of the twentieth century and spread from literary studies to the humanities in the form of the linguistic turn of the second half of that century.[1] The linguistic turn in the humanities was matched by a post-war enthusiasm for humanistic approaches to the social sciences. Qualitative research methods, which sought to privilege rather than eliminate the subjectivity of data, became both more prolific and more respected. Although the structuralist and humanist traditions were at odds in several significant ways, they were sufficiently similar to facilitate a narrative turn in the human sciences as a whole (Squire, Andrews and Tamboukou 2013). Matti Hyvärinen (2010) identifies four distinct stages within this turn, beginning with literary studies in the nineteen sixties, moving to historiography in the nineteen seventies, social research in the nineteen eighties, and culture itself in the nineteen nineties.[2] Catherine Kohler Riessman (2002) explores the turn in more detail, noting the influence of narrative beyond the disciplines of anthropology, psychology, sociolinguistics, and sociology to the professions of law, medicine, nursing, occupational therapy, and social work in the last two decades of the century. As the century changed, the concept of narrative identity – of personality as reducible to or dependent upon autobiographical narrative representation or autobiographical narrative thinking – was adopted by numerous disciplines (Polkinghorne 1988; McAdams 1993).

Criminology has been slow to embrace narrative as a tool for understanding, explaining, and reducing crime and social harm. The initial criminological interest in narrative representation was nonetheless very early, developed in the Department of Sociology at the University of Chicago and focused on the life history. The first sociological life history was William Thomas and Florian Znaniecki's (1927) *The Polish Peasant in Europe and America* (first published from 1918 to 1920 in five volumes and then in 1927 in two volumes) and the first to take crime as its subject, Clifford Shaw's (1930) *The Jack-Roller: A Delinquent Boy's Own Story. The Jack-Roller* is the life history of 'Stanley' (a pseudonym), a twenty-two-year-old man from Chicago with a long record of delinquency from the ages of six to sixteen. Just over half of the book is composed of Stanley's own narrative representation of the sequence of events of his life up to his release from the House of Correction aged seventeen and eight months, as recorded by Shaw in a series of personal interviews. In his introduction to the 1966 edition of *The Jack-Roller*, Howard Becker notes how the use of the life history was encouraged by first Robert E. Park and then Ernest W. Burgess at the University of Chicago. Shaw published subsequent life histories, as did several of his colleagues, including Edwin Sutherland (Conwell and Sutherland 1937). Following a discussion of the sociological value of *The Jack-Roller* in particular and life histories in general, Becker laments that the method failed to become one of the standard research tools of the discipline. He accounts for this neglect in terms of the growing professionalisation of sociology, one of the consequences of which is an increasing requirement that sociological studies are self-sufficient. This trend 'led people to ignore the other functions of research and, particularly, to ignore the contribution made by one study to an overall research enterprise, even when the study, considered in isolation, produced no definitive results of its own' (Becker 1966: xviii). This concern is reflected in Burgess' (1930) discussion of Shaw's case study, the majority of which is aimed at pointing out the features of Stanley's story that are typical of the boys who appear in Cook County Juvenile Court.

Whether Becker's explanation for the lack of interest in the life history in sociology is correct or not, the parallel lack of interest in criminology is indisputable. There were very few criminological studies that employed narrative research methods in the second half of the twentieth century, with three notable exceptions: Henry Williamson and Lincoln Keiser's (1965) *Hustler!*, Lawrence Wieder's (1974) *Language and Social Reality: The Case of Telling the Convict Code*, and David Canter's (1994) *Criminal Shadows: Inside the Mind of the Serial Killer*. As such, the narrative turn in criminology is a phenomenon of the new century. Three of the most important books in the field were published in its first decade: Shadd Maruna's (2001) *Making Good: How Ex-Convicts Reform and Rebuild Their Lives*, Lois Presser's (2008) *Been a Heavy Life: Stories of Violent Men*, and Sveinung Sandberg and Willy Pedersen's (2009) *Street Capital: Black Cannabis Dealers in a White Welfare State*. Maruna's study of the life narratives of offenders is a direct descendant of Shaw's seminal work of narrative criminology. The second decade of the new century has seen the publication of: Presser's (2013) *Why We Harm*, Thomas Ugelvik's (2014) *Power and Resistance in Prison: Doing Time, Doing Freedom,* Jennifer Fleetwood's (2014) *Drug Mules: Women in the international cocaine trade,* and Presser's (2018) *Inside Story: How Narratives Drive Mass Harm.* As the repetition of her name suggests, Presser (2009: 178) has been – and remains – the leading voice in '*narrative criminology*', which she was first to define. Narrative criminology was established as a subdiscipline within criminology by Presser and Sandberg (2015) with *Narrative Criminology: Understanding Stories of Crime,* an edited collection, and the definitive work on the narrative turn in criminology at the time of writing is *The Emerald Handbook of Narrative Criminology,* edited by Fleetwood, Presser, Sandberg, and Ugelvik (2019). Most recently, narrative criminology has imitated the uroboros,[3] turning back on one of the subdisciplines from which it emerged, cultural criminology, in its appropriation by Avi Brisman (2016, 2019) and others practising green cultural criminology. In this chapter I discuss the relationship between narrative representation and criminology, Presser's narrative criminology, and the relevance of the narrative criminological framework to my criminology of narrative fiction. Before doing so, however, I must distinguish among the different levels of criminological inquiry and clarify the ambiguous and vague terminology employed to describe these levels.

Criminological inquiry: levels, methods, narratives

I distinguish six levels of criminological inquiry in this section – approaches, frameworks, theories, models, methodologies, and methods – and define several of the terms used to describe them. It is important to note at the outset that many of these terms are used in different ways by social scientists and that my intention is to establish a taxonomy within which I can examine, compare, and contrast historical and contemporary criminological inquiry into narrative representation and fiction rather than to reconfigure principles of research or reinvent the language of research. Although I have already used the word more broadly in Chapter 1, I begin with *approach,* which I take to denote a set of ontological and epistemological assumptions about social science research. Ontology is the study of what exists, the way in which existing things exist, and how best to classify and codify existing things. Epistemology is the study of what is known, how it is known, and what can be known. Following Jon Frauley (2010), I identify three distinct approaches to criminology as practised as a discrete discipline within the social sciences: positivism (also called naturalism and, somewhat confusingly, realism), constructionism (which should not be confused with constructivism and is also called interpretivism), and realism (which should not be confused with the framework that underpins both left and right realism in criminology). These three approaches combine assumptions about what is being studied in criminology with assumptions about what can be discovered by criminologists.

Positivism is often contrasted with relativism: positivism holds that social scientific theories are accepted in virtue of independent reasoning and relativism that they are accepted in virtue of the conventions of a particular approach (Perri 6 and Bellamy 2011). *Positivism* as employed by Frauley, Nicole Rafter (2006), and as I shall use the term, is an approach to criminology that assumes the social world is an external reality, that social facts have a truth value (that is, can be true or false), and that researchers can access the reality and discover the truth values. The second approach, constructionism, must be distinguished from constructivism. Constructivism usually refers to a psychological theory of conceptual learning, but can – confusingly – also refer to ideational constructionism. Constructionism has three distinct denotations, the theses that: (1) an individual's psychology exerts a significant influence on individual action and social organisation; (2) social institutions are entirely reliant upon consent for their existence; or (3) ideas and beliefs exert a significant influence on the creation of social institutions (ideational constructionism) (Perri 6 and Bellamy 2011). *Constructionism* as employed by Rafter – referred to as interpretivism by Frauley – and as I shall use the term, is an approach to criminology that draws on (1), assuming that the social world is experienced as an external reality, but that researchers can only observe and describe the experience, in consequence of which social facts do not have a truth value. In other words, social facts are constituted by multiple subjective realities, including that of the researcher, and the study of the social world is the study of the intersubjective experience of the world rather than the world itself. The third approach, realism, is (also somewhat confusingly) identified with the critical tradition within criminology by Frauley (2010). Clarification is required as Frauley regards realism as a third way between positivism and constructionism, distinguishing his and Vincenzo Ruggiero's (2003) work from the constructionism of Rafter and cultural criminology. *Realism* as employed by Frauley and as I shall use it here is an approach to criminology that assumes the social world is an external reality and that social facts have a truth value, but that researchers have only partial access to reality, in consequence of which criminological knowledge is approximate to rather than correspondent with reality. While criminologists are unable to reach the truth, they can nonetheless advance the discipline with more accurate approximations of that truth (Perri 6 and Bellamy 2011).

A *framework* (also called a paradigm) is a shared commitment about what research questions are important, what data are relevant, how that data should be interpreted, and what counts as a satisfying answer (Perri 6 and Bellamy 2011). A *theory* refers to a coherent set of propositions that determine the assumptions upon which research is based and the context within which the research is undertaken (McGregor 2018b). Though the denotation of methodology is neither intricate nor abstruse it is frequently used incorrectly, most often as a synonym for method. Methodology does involve method, but has two other components, theory and rationale. A rationale is an exposition of the principles employed in research and of their implications for the method or methods selected. A *method* is the combination of techniques and procedures used to gather and analyse data for research. These three elements are combined in a *methodology*, which is a theory of research, a set of principles, and a system of methods regulating a particular inquiry or a discipline more generally (McGregor 2018b). Finally, a *model* is a formal representation of the realisation of a theory that describes both the method and hypothesis of the research (Perri 6 and Bellamy 2011).[4] Theories can be realised in multiple models, and are, in turn, underpinned and informed by frameworks. Presser's narrative criminology, on which I focus in the remainder of this chapter, is most accurately described as a framework. My criminology of narrative fiction is a theory. Prior to the recent narrative turn in the discipline the main intersection between criminological inquiry and narrative representation was at the level of methods – of both data collection and data analysis.

With respect to data collection, research methods are divided into qualitative and quantitative categories. Qualitative methods are often associated with constructionism and quantitative methods with positivism, but there is no necessary relation between the methods and the approaches. Similarly, narrative representation is usually but not necessarily associated with qualitative research methods, specifically the use of the interview. Unlike the life history, the interview has long been a standard research tool in sociology – *the* standard tool in the opinion of Mark Benney and Everett Hughes, who defined sociology as the science of the interview in a special edition of *The American Journal of Sociology* dedicated to that science in 1956. In interviews, there is a conspicuous tendency for interviewees to represent their experiences as narratives and this storytelling imperative can be either encouraged or suppressed by interviewers (Mishler 1986). Interviews aimed at collecting life histories from interviewees are specifically designed to elicit narratives, using open questions but providing sufficient structure upon which to base an autobiographical account of events (Hollway and Jefferson 2000). Sandra Elliott (2005) discusses the relationship between narrative representation and two quantitative methods of data collection, event histories and life course research. She defines event histories as 'a longitudinal record of *when* particular events have occurred for an individual' (Elliott 2005: 65). Event histories have narrativity, but Elliott notes the absence of closure, in consequence of which they are more accurately described as minimal rather than exemplary narratives. Life course research aims to 'understand individuals' lives through time and in particular to link historical context and social structure to the unfolding of people's lives' (Elliott 2005: 72). Elliott (2005) argues that narrative can provide a foundation for the combination of qualitative and quantitative research, suggesting a mixed methods approach to data collection that integrates event histories with the construction of identity. I discuss narrative identity later.

With respect to data analysis, narrative representation is employed as a method of analysing both qualitative and quantitative data. Elliott Mishler (1995) divides the narrative analysis of qualitative data into three categories, distinguished by their focus on one of the following: narrative content (the description or evaluation of experiences), narrative form (the way in which the story is structured), or narrative context (the production, consumption, and function of stories). I return to narrative form and narrative content later, in my discussion of Presser. *The Jack-Roller* is an example of a substantive narrative analysis and Shaw (1930: 3) describes the value of the analysis of Stanley's life history as the revelation of: '(1) the point of view of the delinquent; (2) the social and cultural situation to which the delinquent is responsive; and (3) the sequence of past experiences and situations in the life of the delinquent.'[5] Formal narrative analysis focuses on the structure of narrative representations and one of the most-cited methods is that of William Labov and Joshua Waletzky (1967). Their sociolinguistic structural model analyses narratives in terms of six formal properties: abstract, orientation, complicating action, evaluation, resolution, and coda. Contextual narrative analysis can focus on either the interaction between individuals as they tell stories or on the role of narratives in society more generally. Kenneth Plummer's (1994) sociological analysis is an example of the latter, employing the concept of genre to demonstrate the function of stories in political transformation. The narrative analysis of quantitative data has for the most part been concerned with event history modelling: modelling strategies applied to event history data in order to determine variables that are relevant to the event in question (Elliott 2005). Elliott (2005) distinguishes two types of event history analysis, continuous time and discrete time. Continuous time focuses on the interval between two events and discrete time on a single event as occurring within an interval (for example, in a particular month or a particular year). Elliott (2005: 87) claims that discrete time provides a greater focus on temporality than continuous time and can, in consequence, be considered as a narrative method of analysis: 'each sequence can potentially be given coherence by the unity of the individual case, and a conclusion or resolution to each narrative is provided by the occurrence (or non-occurrence) of the dependent event.'

Narrative criminological framework

Presser and Sandberg (2015a: 1) define narrative criminology broadly, as 'any inquiry based on the view of stories as instigating, sustaining, or effecting desistance from harmful action'. Although this is both clear and concise, it fails to indicate the level – or levels – of criminological inquiry at which narrative criminology functions. In the two books she has published since coining the term, Presser refers to narrative criminology as criminology 'where the main explanatory variable is one's story' (2013: 29) and as 'the study of the relationship between narratives and harmful actions and patterns' (2018: 2). Sveinung Sandberg (2010), Sandberg and Thomas Ugelvik (2016), and Presser and Sandberg (2019) all refer to narrative criminology as a *framework* and this is the most useful way to conceive of this particular subdiscipline of criminological inquiry, as a shared commitment about what research questions are important, what data are relevant, how that data should be interpreted, and what counts as a satisfying answer. This shared commitment includes story as one of the main explanatory variables in criminology, the relevance of stories to the causes of crime and social harm, and the relevance of stories to desistance from crime and social harm. My criminology of narrative fiction shares these commitments.

In a parallel with Hyvärinen (2010) on the narrative turn in the human sciences, Presser and Sandberg (2015a) identify four theoretical traditions from which narrative criminology developed: narrative psychology, ethnomethodology, cultural structuralism, and postmodernism. Narrative psychology and cultural structuralism can be understood as frameworks, ethnomethodology as a methodology, and postmodernism as an approach (usually considered similar to or identical with relativism as previously defined). Presser and Sandberg (2015a: 11) claim that:

> These four theoretical traditions bring important insights
> to bear on narrative criminology. Narrative psychology

reminds us that a speaker is an agent who seeks coherence, ethnomethodology that speakers use narratives as devices in particular social contexts, cultural structuralism that narration is essentially reproductive, and postmodernism that narratives are often fragmented and hybrid.

Presser and Sandberg move on to discuss two related criminological traditions (which, again, can be understood as frameworks), constitutive criminology and cultural criminology. The relationships among the narrative, constitutive, and cultural frameworks of criminology raise the question of the approach to criminological inquiry that informs narrative criminology, which does not admit of a straightforward answer. Presser and Sandberg pay the constitutive criminological framework and the cultural criminological framework equal attention, but I shall focus on the cultural criminological framework on the basis that it is more popular amongst criminologists, has a more direct link to narrative criminology, and has relevance for my criminology of narrative fiction.

Cultural criminology emerged from the subcultural theories developed by sociologists such as Albert Cohen (1955) and David Matza (1964) and the work of Stuart Hall and his collaborators at first the University of Birmingham (Hall et al. 1978) and then the Open University (Hall, Evans and Nixon 1997) on media, representation, and meaning. The framework was pioneered by Jeff Ferrell (1996) and Keith Hayward (2004) and concentrated on culture as the site of meaning-making and as a tool for intervention in the politics of crime control. Ferrell (1999: 396) describes the cultural criminological framework as 'an emergent array of perspectives linked by sensitivities to image, meaning, and representation in the study of crime and crime control'. According to Ferrell, Hayward, and Jock Young (2015), cultural criminology is essentially concerned with the interweaving of cultural forces with the practices of crime and its control and aims to: understand crime as expressive; understand crime as a global public spectacle, mediated for consumption; and provide a critique of the politics of crime and criminal justice. Rafter (2006: 5) claims that cultural criminology has the potential to breach the division between the disciplines of film studies and criminology and characterises the framework as 'a new area of inquiry that aims at understanding how social groups perceive and create knowledge about crime'. Frauley (2010) acknowledges a twofold debt to cultural criminology in developing his theory of the criminological significance of cinematic fictions: taking popular culture as an object of study and taking representations as the focus of analysis. He maintains that both Rafter's theory, which also concerns the criminological significance of cinematic fictions, and the cultural criminological framework are constructionist and Rafter appears to concur with Frauley's categorisations.

Frauley (2010: 55) understands constructionism as an approach that cannot reach beyond the 'textual image' – that is, beyond the representation itself, which can only provide knowledge of the cultural conceptions of crime and criminals and the ideas and assumptions of the creator of the representation. Cultural criminology is primarily concerned with collective expression (cultural conceptions) and Rafter with both collective and individual expression (the director of a film). In other words, cultural criminologists restrict their research to the production and reception of representations rather than to the reality represented. Ferrell's (1995: 29) initial description of the relationship between representation and reality refers to mirroring: 'as cultural criminologists, we study not only images, but images of images, an infinite hall of mediated mirrors.' Ferrell, Hayward, and Young (2015: 155) develop this conception, which is:

> a circulating cultural fluidity that challenges any certain distinction between an event and its representation, a mediated image and its effects, a criminal moment and its ongoing construction within collective meaning. Importantly, this looping process suggests for us something more than Baudrillard's postmodern hyper-reality, his sense of an "unreality" defined only by media images and obfuscation. Quite the opposite: we mean to suggest a late-modern world in which the gritty, on-the-ground reality of crime, violence and everyday criminal justice is dangerously confounded with its own representation.[6]

There is an obvious affinity between cultural criminology and narrative criminology in that many of the representations with which cultural criminology is concerned are narrative representations, whether descriptive, depictive, or – as is increasingly often the case – a hybrid of the two. There is, in consequence, a sizable area of overlap between the two frameworks and Presser and Sandberg (2015a) distinguish narrative criminology from cultural criminology on the basis of narrative criminology's explicit focus on discourse and the language of which it is composed.

The constitutive criminological framework was established by Stuart Henry and Dragan Milovanovic (1996) with *Constitutive*

Criminology: Beyond Postmodernism. Constitutive criminology concentrates on the co-production of crime rather than the cause of crime, where co-production is conceived as the energisation of social structure and group culture by the individual subject. Presser and Sandberg (2015a) differentiate narrative criminology from constitutive criminology on the basis of constitutive criminology's explicit rejection of the realist tradition of criminology. And this is where identifying the approach upon which the narrative criminological framework is based becomes complicated. On the first page of their introduction, shortly after the definition of narrative criminology quoted previously, Presser and Sandberg (2015a: 1) state: 'The approach is a constructionist one.' This is consistent with Presser's (2008) initial monograph, *Been a Heavy Life*, which is based on the life stories of 27 violent men, collected by means of a series of interviews conducted from April 1999 to August 2001. Presser (2008: 10) states of this research: 'I adopt a "post-positivist" perspective on narratives that takes the assertion, that all documentation/knowledge is partial, even further. According to this perspective, narrative is seen as *constitutive* of reality – not as its representation.' She also refers to the co-production of the data acquired through these interviews, drawing attention to the need for reflexivity in a researcher. The complication arises in that Presser and Sandberg (2015a: 12) describe their approach as realist later in the same introduction: 'in its explicit concern to distinguish causes of crime, narrative criminology stands within the realist tradition of the discipline.' This raises the question of whether the narrative criminological framework is based upon a constructionist or realist approach as – in the terminology I am using – it cannot be both.

The answer lies in the varied and vague employment of the terms in question by researchers working across different disciplines – and even within a single discipline – that necessitated the creation of a taxonomy in the first instance. Presser (2008: 10) suggests this answer herself in *Been a Heavy Life* when she quotes Burgess' (1930: 189) commentary on *The Jack-Roller*: ' "In human affairs it is not the absolute truth about an event that concerns us but the way in which persons react to that event." ' At the methodological level, Presser (2008) is concerned with self-presentation by her interviewees, not with the accuracy of their personal histories, that is with narratives as constitutive rather than representative (a distinction I discuss later). The care that Presser takes to focus on the way in which the interviewees experience the social world and the way in which their life stories are co-produced in the context of the interviews is consistent with the constructionist approach. Recall, however, that realism charts an approach between positivism and constructionism, assuming that the social world is an external reality and that social facts have a truth value, but that researchers have only partial access to reality. This is consistent with Presser's claims to post-positivism and partial knowledge and Presser and Sandberg's location of the narrative criminological framework within the realist tradition. Realism as an approach to criminological inquiry is not inconsistent with the focus on narratives as constitutive and Presser (2018: 14) gestures towards the different levels in her third monograph, *Inside Story*:

> The supposed falsehood of certain stories has, in my view, been a distraction to narrative inquiry within criminology (Presser 2016). It has been presumed that only "real" things cause crime. Hence, many analysts who collect and/or appreciate narrative data seek to verify the authenticity of what the narrator has reported. But narratives affect us whether or not they are true.

Presser's interest is in reality – causes of crime and narrative effects – not just the representation of that reality in stories. Representations (life stories, memoirs, autobiographies) are real whether or not they are accurate and narrative criminology takes the impact of narrative representations as its subject rather than their truth value. Narrative criminology is thus a framework within the realist approach and this realism distinguishes the narrative criminological framework from the constructionist approach of both the cultural and the constitutive criminological frameworks. The approach in my criminology of narrative fiction is realist rather than constructionist, which provides further evidence for a close relationship between my theory and the narrative criminological framework

Constitutive narratives

Presser's development of the narrative criminological framework is evinced in the core theses of each of her monographs. *Been a Heavy Life* (Presser 2008) draws on both Mills (1940) and Maruna (2001) to argue that life stories construct personal identity and that the construction of personal identity enables all action, including harmful action. Presser (2008: 14) identifies three narrative structures that the men in her study employ to underpin future action, including both desistance and violence: '*reform* – actually, a return to moral decency or constant moral decency – *stability* – as well as a hybrid or *elastic* structure that combined talk about self-reform and self-stability.' *Why We Harm* (Presser 2013) establishes a 'narrative criminology of harm', in which she (Presser 2013: 17) analyses the apparently varied harms of genocide, the consumption of nonhuman animals, intimate partner violence, and incarceration. Presser (2013: 109) discloses the significance of narrative representation to all of these harms as well as to harm in general: 'We do harm because of cultural logics, typically in the form of stories, that reduce the target of harm and conjure ourselves as both authorized to harm and powerless not to.' *Inside Story* (Presser 2018) is her most ambitious work yet, a sociology of mass harm that attempts to explain the way in which narrative representation impacts aggregates, contributing to the global phenomenon of mass harm. Presser (2018) argues that underdog stories (a version of which is delineated in *Been a Heavy Life*) and stories that immobilise agency (a development of the cultural logics of *Why We Harm*) authorise and promote mass harm. She then differentiates between bounded narratives and notional narratives (a distinction that runs parallel to my exemplary narratives and minimal narratives) and claims that notional narratives have greater sociological significance because of the ease with which they can be reproduced, reiterated, and redistributed by social and mass media. With respect to the reduction of mass harm: 'Both kinds of examination are important, but I believe that a cultural sociology of contemporary mass harm is in greater need of the latter because the most pervasive and impactful narratives are notional' (Presser 2018: 140).

Presser (2016) characterises her framework – and that of narrative criminology more generally – as being distinct from previous intersections of narrative representation and criminological inquiry in virtue of two features. First, narrative criminology focuses on the form of narratives rather than their content. Across all modes of representation, the form of a particular representation can be distinguished from the content of that representation and this form-content pairing is also referred to as style-substance, manner-matter, and medium-message. The importance of this relationship has been recognised for more than two millennia, with Plato (1997) differentiating the style of stories from their content in the *Republic*. The literary critical interest in the relationship that would prove so influential in the twentieth century was initiated with A.C. Bradley's (1901) inaugural lecture at Oxford, "Poetry for Poetry's Sake", in which he sketched an argument for the value of the experience of poetry on the basis of the integration of poetic form and poetic content in that experience. In linguistic or descriptive representation form includes: structure, morphology (the patterns of word formation), syntax (the rules of sentence formation), metre (the arrangement of words in regularly measured, patterned, or rhythmic lines or verses), and tropes (all literary or rhetorical devices that use words in other than their literal sense). Content includes subject, theme, characters, settings, and actions (McGregor 2016). Unlike form, content remains constant throughout different modes of representation. Form in pictorial or depictive representation includes: line, shape (a two-dimensional closed line), form (a three-dimensional shape), colour, and texture (Gombrich 1950). Form in hybrid modes of representation combines elements from the discrete modes of representation with elements unique to the compounding of those modes. In cinematic representation the convention is to distinguish film form from film style, where film form refers to the formal elements associated with a film as a narrative and film style to the formal elements associated with the technology required to animate pictures. Film form includes genre, structure, function, and framework. Film style includes *mise-en-scène*, cinematography, editing, and sound (Bordwell, Thompson and Smith 2017).[7] Although 'narrative representation' is often employed as if it is a mode of representation, 'narrative' is more accurately understood as a formal element, as narrative form is imposed upon a substantive sequence of events. Narrative form in this sense is often referred to as *plot* and *emplotment* is the process of representing a sequence of events as a narrative. I shall follow Bradley (who in turn follows Plato) in providing a simple definition of *form* as how a representation represents and *content* as what a representation represents. Presser's claim is thus that the way in which a story is told has more sociological significance than what happens in the story. My criminology of narrative fiction aligns closely with this feature of the narrative criminological framework, but not completely: where Presser emphasises narrative form at the expense of narrative content, I regard the pair as equally significant.

Presser's focus on form underpins the second distinctive feature of the narrative criminological framework, which treats narratives as constitutive rather than representational: stories are regarded as shaping experience rather than providing evidence of events or evidence of the way in which events are experienced. Presser and Sandberg (2015a) draw on Paul Ricoeur's (1983, 1984, 1985) account of the relationship between narrative and reality as threefold – objective, subjective, and constitutive – in order to explain this feature. In the first relation, narratives are regarded as transparent, as objective representations of reality. In the second, narratives are opaque, subjective representations of the experience of reality. In the third, narratives are performative, having a reciprocal relationship with experience such that narratives both produce experience and are the product of experience. Presser

(2016) refers to the first two of these categories as a representational conception of narrative and the third as a constitutive conception of narrative. While she neither denies nor discards the representational conception, she characterises the narrative criminological framework in terms of the constitutive conception. Presser (2008, 2009, 2013) explores this constitutivity in terms of personal identity, which is first an internal narrative and second a self-story that conditions future actions. The relationship between internal narrative and future action employs Donald Polkinghorne's (1988) exploration of the narrative understanding of personal identity. Polkinghorne also draws on Ricoeur and argues that temporality is the most significant dimension of human existence. Temporal experience is configured into past, present, and future, but human beings strive to create meaning by establishing relations between the parts (disconnected events) and the whole (totality of an individual's experience). This is achieved by narrative configuration, which not only unifies the events by means of themes, but directs them towards a conclusion: the emplotment that transforms a sequence of events into a narrative representation also transforms an experienced sequence of events into a narrative identity. In this way, 'the unity and uniqueness of the self is achieved through the process of narrativity' (Polkinghorne 1988: 151).

Dan McAdams (2015) describes a similar process, in which human beings strive to first find a pattern in their lives and then to attribute some kind of meaning to that pattern. In other words, human beings strive to impose narrative order on what would otherwise be a series of disconnected and contingent events. He (McAdams 2015: 250) defines narrative identity as: 'the internalized and evolving story of the self that a person constructs to provide his or her life with unity, purpose, and meaning'. Narrative identity is a myth created by the individual that provides meaning rather than truth, but McAdams argues that this function makes it more rather than less compelling in motivating behaviour – all of which is consistent with Presser's constitutive conception of narratives. Narrative configuration structures previous action retrospectively and determines future action because emplotment involves progression from the past through the present towards an anticipated or imagined future. Polkinghorne (1988: 150) describes this process as dynamic rather than static: 'We are in the middle of our stories and cannot be sure how they will end; we are constantly having to revise the plots as new events are added to our lives.' Each time narrative configuration occurs, it influences both the past and the future. Presser and Sandberg (2015a: 1) articulate the consequences of this crucial continuity at the beginning of their introduction to *Narrative Criminology*: 'Our self-stories condition what we will do tomorrow because whatever tomorrow brings, our responses must somehow cohere with the storied identity generated thus far.' Narratives thus constitute rather than represent the causes of crime and social harm. Presser's core claim is that internal narratives provide an understanding of the causes of crime and social harm by explaining future actions as either realising or advancing the individual or collective narratives of offenders. This explanation is made in virtue of the fact that personal identity is created and maintained by means of narrative configuration. In contrast, although I recognise the value of the constitutive conception of narrative, my criminology of narrative fiction employs the representational conception exclusively. Given the significance of the constitutive conception to the narrative criminological framework, my criminology of narrative fiction is best understood as a theory that is emergent from rather than situated within that framework.

Moral stories

In *Narrative Justice* (McGregor 2018b), which I discuss in Chapter 3, I argue that narrative representation is essentially ethical on the basis that both narrativity and ethical value are concerned with the combination of agency and event. Wherever there is an agent who acts that agent can be judged for their action (or inaction) and in moral philosophy this judgement is usually based on one or more of: the agent's motive for the action, features of the action itself, or the consequences of the action. All action (and inaction) can be evaluated as one of: morally permissible, morally prohibited, or morally obligatory. All narrative representations involve at least one agent and two events and are thus also necessarily subject to ethical evaluation. The consequence of this relation between narrativity and ethical value is that every story does indeed have a moral – that is, ethical value – but the moral can be virtuous, vicious, or somewhere in between. Presser (2009) reaches a similar conclusion by different means, employing the concept of narrative distance. She argues that the act of narrating a self-story creates a distinction between the present narrator and the past protagonist, even though they are identical. Presser draws on Charlotte Linde's (1993) sociolinguistic study of life stories, which proposes a fundamental relation between reflexivity and morality. For Linde, the act of the narrator's commentary on herself as a protagonist exploits the distance between protagonist and narrator to establish the narrator as a moral agent (regardless of whether the protagonist is represented as moral or amoral). Presser's (2009: 180) take on this narrative distance is that 'a person's narrative presupposes a moral self in the narrating present'. The importance of this presupposition is evinced in her research in *Been a Heavy Life* (Presser 2008). In the reform narratives, offenders distance the amoral protagonist from the moral narrator, emphasising transition from the former to the latter. In the stability narratives, offenders portray a consistent moral self, describing acts of violence as either necessary or as temporary (and insignificant) lapses in character. The most common plot underpinning the reform, stability, and elastic narrative structures is that of the heroic struggle, of the protagonist striving against the odds to overcome marginalisation and injustice.

Why We Harm (Presser 2013) turns Presser's narrative criminology away from internal narratives towards the relationship between narratives of the self and narratives of others: the stories that tell people who they are and the stories that tell people who others are. The cultural logics that establish this relationship produce harm by providing three types of motivation. The first focuses on the target of the harm and recalls Gresham Sykes and David Matza's (1957) neutralisation techniques. The target is reduced in some way, either by the reduction of moral status – such as the representation of enemies as immoral (and thus deserving of harm) – or a denial that actual harm occurred. Both of these devices typically involve the representation of the target as having less complexity than the perpetrator of the harm. The second and third types of motivation focus on the perpetrator, as either powerful or powerless. In the second, the perpetrator is represented as being licensed to commit certain harms. This licence is granted by a wide variety of circumstances, which include the absence of sanctions, the presence of opportunities, and even the availability of means. The licence both empowers the perpetrator and confers some type of authority on her. In direct contrast, the third type of motivation represents the perpetrator as powerless, as the target of marginalisation and injustice, in consequence of which she has no option but to perpetrate harm (which may also be represented as heroic struggle). The second and third motivations are not mutually exclusive and Presser (2013: 117) claims that the 'power paradox' – the peculiar combination of power and powerlessness found in perpetrators of harm – has the potential to motivate the perpetration of harm by both individuals and organisations in a variety of ways. The three cultural logics that motivate harm fit neatly into the three categories of moral evaluation: the representation of the target as reduced makes harm morally permissible; the licensing of harm allows the perpetrator to ignore moral prohibitions; and the representation of the perpetrator as powerless makes harm morally obligatory.

Inside Story (Presser 2018) continues the trajectory of Presser's sociology of harm from the internal to the external, from acts of violence to the phenomenon of mass harm. She argues that some narratives are particularly well-attuned to the moral aspect of lived experience and that these narratives arouse intense emotional responses. The combination of form and content in narrative representation in terms of features such as figurativeness and ambiguity invite active engagement with the narrative by the audience, to make sense of the story by means of either interpretation or evaluation.[8] For Presser (2018), the emotional responses relevant to mass harm are moral outrage and moral satisfaction. Underdog stories (a shared version of the heroic struggle internal narrative) provoke outrage, invite action, and motivate mass violence. Hegemonic stories provoke satisfaction in audiences by representing the audience as virtuous and, in consequence, sustain structural violence. With respect to the actual impact of narratives on the perpetration of harm (their causal effect), the most important category is the notional narrative (where no authoritative version or stable text exists). Notional narratives may be based on or derived from the more traditional bounded narratives (where an authoritative version does exist), but have greater impact because of the extent to which they are created, consumed, recreated, and communicated by social and mass media. In other words, notional narratives are better vehicles for provoking moral outrage and moral satisfaction than bounded narratives and, in consequence, cause more mass harm.

In the final chapter of *Been a Heavy Life*, Presser (2008) asks whether heroism is criminogenic. Her answer is in the affirmative, on the basis that the heroic struggle plot is intimately tied to the culturally dominant model of masculine identity and an essential aspect of doing masculinity. Putting all three of her monographs in perspective, one might ask whether moral selfhood is criminogenic or, more significantly for Presser (2018: 2), 'harmgenic'. The answer is clearly also in the affirmative. At the level of the internal narrative, the heroic struggle justifies the perpetration of harm by representing that struggle as being morally obligatory. At the level of narratives that determine the relationship between self and other, cultural logics classify harm as either morally permissible (by reducing the target or licensing the perpetrator) or morally obligatory (the powerless perpetrator). At the level of narratives that motivate collective violence, the provocation of moral emotions in the audience frames mass harm as either morally obligatory (moral outrage) or morally permissible (moral satisfaction). The relationship between constitutive narratives and moral selfhood is thus crucial to Presser's project. In contrast, my criminology of narrative fiction is primarily concerned with the knowledge provided by narrative representations and while some of this knowledge is concerned with ethical questions, neither morality nor moral selfhood make a significant contribution to the theory. This difference provides further evidence for conceiving of my theory as emergent from rather than situated within the narrative criminological framework.

Conclusion

I began this chapter with a brief history of the structural turn in literary criticism, the linguistic turn in the humanities, the narrative turn in the human sciences, and the more recent narrative turn in criminology. In order to avoid confusion amongst the different forms that the criminological interest in narrative representation has taken, I distinguished six levels of research: approaches, frameworks, theories, models, methodologies, and methods. With this taxonomy in place, I summarised the qualitative and quantitative narrative methods of data collection and data analysis that are employed in criminology. I identified Presser (2008, 2013, 2018) as the leading voice in the subdiscipline of narrative criminology and located that subdiscipline with respect to other subdisciplines and the discipline as a whole. I argued that both cultural criminology and narrative criminology are best understood as criminological frameworks, that is as shared commitments about what research questions are important, what data are relevant, how that data should be interpreted, and what counts as a satisfying answer. I then argued that these frameworks could be distinguished on the basis of their different approaches to research. Cultural criminology is a constructionist framework, assuming that the study of the social world is the study of the intersubjective experience of reality rather than reality itself. Narrative criminology is a realist framework, assuming that the study of the social world is the study of reality, but that researchers have only partial access to that reality.

With these classifications in place, I examined Presser's research in more detail, drawing attention to the two features that differentiate the narrative criminological framework from the previous intersections of criminological inquiry and narrative representation. First, narrative criminology regards the form of narratives as more significant than their content, focusing on the way in which stories are told rather than what happens in those stories. Second, and related, narrative criminology regards the constitutive conception of narratives as more significant than the representational conception, focusing on narratives as performative, as both producing and being produced by human experience.

Crucial to this focus is the narrative configuration of identity, which retrospectively imposes meaning on the sequence of events of one's life and motivates future action by establishing anticipated or imagined conclusions. After summarising Presser's work on internal narratives, narratives that determine the relationship between the self and others, and narratives that motivate mass harm, I identified the significance of moral selfhood to narrative explanations of harm. The heroic struggle, cultural logics, and provocation of moral emotions all justify harm or mass harm as either morally obligatory or morally permissible.

There are notable differences between my criminology of narrative fiction and the narrative criminological framework, but the similarities are too significant to ignore and my debt to Presser is obvious. With this play of identity and difference in mind, I suggested that my theory should be regarded as emergent from rather than situated within the narrative criminological framework. Most importantly, I share the core commitments of narrative criminology: to story as one of the main explanatory variables in criminology, to the relevance of stories to the causes of crime and social harm, and to the relevance of stories to desistance from crime and social harm. Second, my approach is also realist, assuming that the social world is an external reality and that social facts have a truth value, but that researchers have only partial access to reality. Third, I share an emphasis on narrative form with Presser, although unlike her emphasis of form at the expense of content my emphasis is divided equally between the pairing. There are also three differences between Presser's framework and my theory, which stretch the relation between the two. First, Presser's research is exclusively concerned with nonfictional narratives (despite her lack of interest in their truth value or representational content) whereas mine is exclusively concerned with fictional narratives. Second, my conception of narrative is representational where Presser's is constitutive. Finally, my theory does not share Presser's emphasis on morality and moral selfhood in her framework. Ultimately, it does not matter whether my criminology of narrative fiction is classified as being part of or emergent from narrative criminology. What does matter is that I have positioned my research in relation to the narrative criminological framework and, in so doing, set out my assumptions and commitments. The next step, which I undertake in Chapter 3, is to position my research with respect to the existing criminological engagements with narrative fiction.

3

Fictional Criminologies

Introduction

The first module I ever led was in the 2011/2012 academic year at a college that taught degrees awarded by a university that has since changed its name, as part of an honours degree in policing and community studies that no longer exists. 'Community & Diversity' was a final year module with two learning outcomes, concerning prejudice and cohesion. Being new to both the programme and module leadership, I followed my predecessor's scheme of learning, which organised the 30 weeks of teaching around eight topics: multi-agency policing, social identity, policing hard to reach groups, social exclusion, multiculturalism, equality of opportunity, the politics of policing, and the role of gender. As most of the 27 students in the class had enrolled on the programme with the intention of pursuing a career in the criminal justice system, I thought it was important to emphasise police practice and made extensive use of case studies and student debates, both enhanced by audio-visual means, mostly short clips from documentaries, television, or films. I was particularly keen to convey the difficulties of policing 'hard to reach groups', communities where relationships with the police are either strained or antagonistic. Having had some experience of this aspect of policing in my own career in law enforcement, the obvious choice was to introduce narratives of that experience into the relevant lectures, but I worried that these would be lost amidst the rest of the lecture and fail to communicate what it is like to police a community in which one is not welcome.[1] Instead, I created five scenarios loosely based on my experiences, where I described a situation in detail and asked students to discuss: how they thought they would respond; how they thought police officers should respond; and how they thought the police officers had responded. Once the groups had presented their answers to the class, I described the actual response and turned the discussion to the reasons for the discrepancies between preferred and actual responses. Overall, I was happy with the lesson, but I felt that I could have conveyed the challenges of this aspect of policing in a more memorable manner and intended to revise the lesson plan the following year.

In consequence of the delivery of the programme being changed from full time to part time the module did not run in 2012/2013. As the first term of that year came to an end, David Ayer's *End of Watch* (2012) was released in the UK. The film follows the day-to-day lives of two officers in the Los Angeles Police Department, Brian Taylor (played by Jake Gyllenhaal) and Miguel Zavala (played by Michael Peña), as they patrol Newton division in South Central Los Angeles, an area notorious for its violent crime, which is for the most part perpetrated by street gangs. The narrative opens with a high-speed car chase that ends in a shootout between Taylor and Zavala and two gangsters, all viewed through the dashboard camera of the police car. Ayer deliberately blurs the line between fiction and documentary by making additional use of scenes that appear to be have been filmed by cameras held by characters on the screen. The representation of policing a hard to reach community is very realistic and Taylor and Zavala are so successful in disrupting the strongest Sureños gang in Newton that they are targeted for assassination by the Sinaloa Cartel. The conclusion of the narrative is particularly interesting. The sequence of events ends with Zavala's funeral, where a badly wounded Taylor gives an emotional eulogy. The narrative then flashes back to Zavala's last shift, where he tells Taylor an amusing and intimate anecdote involving his parents-in-law. What this closure achieves is to draw attention to the significance of the bond between Taylor and Zavala, which in turn frames them as not only hardworking and courageous, but also affable and compassionate, to the extent that the audience is likely to accept the invitation to approve of their occasionally unorthodox style of policing.

I was immediately struck by the film's pedagogic value. Here was a narrative that represented many of the challenges of policing a hard to reach community and represented these challenges from the point of view (literally in some sequences) of two police officers with whom the majority of the audience would identify. Unlike my previous uses of television or film clips, my idea was to use the whole film as a teaching tool the next year, dividing it into four sections of 25 minutes, each of which would be introduced by me and followed by student discussion of the parts relevant to the module. I did not in fact teach the module again, but I was able to make use of the method in my lifelong learning teaching practice and completed my Professional Graduate Certificate in Education with a study of film as a pedagogic tool.[2] I suspect that no academics would contest the pedagogic potential of cinematic narratives, whether fictional (like *End of Watch*) or nonfictional (like *Waltz with Bashir* and *13th*). There are, however, at least three distinct epistemic roles that narrative fictions can play in criminological inquiry: semiotic, pedagogic, and aetiological. In the *semiotic role*, narrative fictions provide knowledge of the production and reception of representations of crime and its control (Rafter 2006). The *pedagogic role* of narrative fiction is to facilitate, augment, or enhance the communication of criminological knowledge (Atkinson and Beer 2010). Finally, narrative fictions provide knowledge of the causes of crime or social harm in the *aetiological role* (Matthews 2014).

In Chapter 2 I introduced Jon Frauley's (2010) differentiation of his own contribution to the relationship between narrative fiction and criminological inquiry from those of Nicole Rafter (2006) and Vincenzo Ruggiero (2003). Frauley proposes a progression of the treatment of narrative fiction from Rafter's source of student discussion to Ruggeiro's pedagogic and analytic tool to his own development of Ruggiero's framework, in which fictional literary and cinematic realities have pedagogic value in exemplifying concepts and theories and analytic value in providing empirical referents for those concepts and theories. I noted that both Ruggiero and Frauley employ a realist approach to research and Frauley's discussion, analysis, and evaluation of Ruggiero makes it clear that they share the same framework within that approach. Out of deference to Frauley's attempt to link the realist approach to critical criminology as well as the way in which the term is employed in scientific and philosophical inquiry more generally (Bhaskar 1975, 1987, 1989), I shall use *critical realist framework* to describe the commitment about what research questions are important, what data are relevant, how that data should be interpreted, and what counts as a satisfying answer that Ruggiero and Frauley share. This chapter proceeds by distinguishing my criminology of narrative fiction from first the cultural criminological framework, then from the critical realist framework, and finally from my work within the narrative criminological framework (McGregor 2018b). My conclusion is that despite claims to the contrary, none of the previous engagements with narrative fiction have presented a convincing argument for the aetiological role of narrative fiction, that is for narrative fiction as providing knowledge of the causes of crime and social harm.

Cultural criminological framework

Although the cultural criminological framework was the first to take fiction seriously, its treatment of fictional representations has been almost exclusively negative, as the subject of critique. The critical perspective is evident in both of the debts Frauley (2010) acknowledges to cultural criminology, the focus on first popular culture and then on representation. With regard to popular culture, cultural criminologists have attended to what Michelle Brown (2004: 220) calls the 'sizable gap in the field between what criminologists know about crime and what everyone else assumes'. The distinction is between the epistemological expertise of the former and the ideological ignorance of the latter. Rafter (2006: 9) defines *ideology* in terms of the myths that shape social reality, where *myth* is, in turn: 'a descriptive term for the fundamental notions that people hold (usually without much conscious thought) about how the world is structured, what is valuable and unworthy, who is good and who is bad, and which kinds of actions are wrong or right.' As such, the cultural criminological attention to representation has been largely concerned with misrepresentation, with crime fiction as misrepresenting the reality of crime (Reiner 2019). Writing at the turn of the century, David Garland (2001) argued that the mass media had institutionalised a specific view of crime and punishment by means of tabloid news and television fiction, with a culture of control replacing a culture of correctionalism in the US and the UK in a little over two decades. Gray Cavender (2004) accuses Garland of understating the influence of the media, on the basis of televised documentary and drama having produced a mutually-reinforcing flow of information that fashioned the public endorsement of punitive policies. Neither Garland nor Cavender are claiming that the mass media caused high crime rates to become an organising principle of social reality in the nineteen seventies, but that the cultural representations of rising crime both evinced and perpetuated the emergence of a widespread fear of crime.

This reciprocal relationship provides a concrete example of Jeff Ferrell's (1995) infinite hall of mediated mirrors (discussed in Chapter 2). The rising crime rate in the UK from the mid-nineteen fifties and in the US from the mid-nineteen sixties was reflected in the rising popularity of police procedural fiction. The combination of crime fiction and crime news shaped what Garland (2001: 163) calls the 'crime complex of late modernity', which was in turn reflected in the change in crime fiction in the nineteen seventies, with more dangerous criminals requiring more ruthless police officers to maintain public safety. Cultural change in a constant direction over an extended period is more accurately characterised by Ferrell, Hayward, and Young's (2015: 155) cultural looping (also discussed in Chapter 2), where the 'mediated nature of contemporary culture not only carries along the meaning of crime and criminality; it circles back to amplify, distort and define the experience of crime and criminality itself'. Garland (2001) describes the changes in policy and culture from the nineteen sixties to the nineteen nineties as a movement from an ideal of social progress to an ideal of zero tolerance, distorted and amplified through repeated looping to justify a security state built on the twin pillars of market discipline and moral discipline. This is the sense in which Ferrell, Hayward, and Young (2015) are sceptical of both documentary and dramatic representations, as creating a social reality where the gritty, on-the-ground reality of crime, violence, and everyday criminal justice is dangerously confounded with its own representation.

In my discussion of positivism, constructionism, and realism in Chapter 2, I identified the cultural criminological framework as constructionist: assuming that social facts are constituted by multiple subjective realities, including that of the researcher, and that the study of the social world is the study of the intersubjective experience of the world rather than the world itself. The cultural criminological framework can provide knowledge of the production and reception of representations, but it cannot provide knowledge of the reality represented (or misrepresented) by those representations. In other words, narrative fiction can play a semiotic but not an aetiological role in virtue of the constructionist approach underpinning the cultural criminological framework. Although Rafter (2006) shares this constructionist approach, Frauley (2010) claims that she is not working within the cultural criminological framework in consequence of the four types of knowledge she recognises as embedded in the fictional reality of cinematic representations. The first two of these are completely compatible with the cultural criminological framework: 'knowledge of *popular views* on the nature and causes of crime and criminality'; and embodying a '*popularized version of criminological knowledge*' (Frauley 2010: 45). Third, films embody 'knowledge of *how ideology is connected to the power* to shape and mould popular knowledge as well as criminological knowledge' (Frauley 2010: 45). This appears to be a step beyond the cultural criminological framework as although the relationship between ideology and power is a cultural criminological concern, cultural criminologists are more likely to regard a crime film as providing evidence of the operation of that relationship rather than embedding knowledge about it. Fourth, 'films offer *speculative knowledge* about the nature of crime in our society, in future and also past societies' (Frauley 2010: 45). It is not entirely clear whether Frauley uses speculative in its theoretical or conjectural denotation (or both), but he refers to its reception by audiences as potentially indicative of confidence in public policy and academic criminology.

I think Frauley is correct to read Rafter as developing previous cultural criminological work on fiction, but that he errs in identifying her framework as distinct from cultural criminology. Rafter's (2006) theory of crime films as a tool for (1) critical thinking and (2) either reaffirming the moral order or refusing easy solutions was one of the first to treat fiction as facilitating the communication of criminological knowledge (as well as confounding reality with its representation). In Rafter, like Frauley, film provides a means by which the criminological imagination can be exercised, inviting creative and rigorous interpretation that explores the relationships between private and public, agency and structure, and individuals and types. Within green cultural criminology, Avi Brisman (2016, 2019) has recently followed suit, arguing that narrative fictions can enhance the communication of criminological knowledge, especially environmental harm. Similarly, while Gray Cavender and Nancy Jurik (2012: 35) mention neither cultural criminology nor the criminological imagination in *Justice Provocateur: Jane Tennison and Policing in Prime Suspect*, they are clearly conducting their research within the cultural criminological framework and clearly concerned with the criminological imagination, claiming that: 'our model directs attention to how much a cultural product portrays the structural context of individual problems, that is, to what extent it connects personal troubles with public issues.' Cavender and Jurik establish a model of progressive moral fiction, a genre characterised by insight into the experiences of the marginalised, the location of these experiences in a social context, the revelation of fissures in the ruling apparatus, and glimpses of hope to challenge injustice – all of which are represented from the point of view of a *justice provocateur*, an agent for positive change. The examination of the *Prime Suspect* (1991–2006) television series in these terms provides evidence of the model's value as a tool for both the analysis of narrative fiction and for exploring social justice issues with students.

The point I am making with Brisman and Cavender and Jurik is that the cultural criminological framework is not necessarily restricted to a critique of narrative fiction and that Rafter's treatment of crime films as communicating knowledge is therefore insufficient to distinguish her framework from cultural criminology. This knowledge cannot, however, reach beyond the production and reception of the representation to the reality represented and it is significant that Cavender and Jurik's evaluation of their own model is as providing a tool for narrative analysis (analysis of the representation) and a tool for pedagogy, in a more sophisticated but nonetheless similar manner to that which I envisaged for *End of Watch* in my 'Community & Diversity' class. What about Frauley's treatment of the knowledge embedded in the fictional reality of cinematic representation in Rafter? He (Frauley 2010: 45) expands on how ideology is connected to power by stating: 'In this way, film can help us visualize the dialectical interplay between forms of exclusion and the dominantly accepted ideas about crime, criminality, and control.' Crucially, the representation is *helping to visualise* social reality rather than *providing knowledge* thereof, that is augmenting communication about the dialectical interplay. The fourth type of knowledge is *speculative* and although this implies a movement from the representation to the reality, Frauley characterises it as being concerned with the reception of representations. My reading of Rafter is thus that her criminology of crime films is, like Cavender and Jurik's model of progressive moral fiction, located within the cultural criminological framework. Frauley conceives of this framework as being unable to reach beyond the representation to the reality on the grounds that it is underpinned by the constructionist approach. In consequence, theories of narrative fiction within the cultural criminological framework are restricted to the semiotic and pedagogic roles, providing knowledge of the production and reception of representations or facilitating, augmenting, or enhancing the communication of knowledge.

Ruggiero's critical realism

Ruggiero (2003: 1) begins *Crime in Literature: Sociology of Deviance and Fiction* with a clear and succinct statement of his aim: 'This book uses fiction as a tool for the communication of sociological meaning and the elaboration of criminological analysis. It addresses the issues of crime and crime control through the reading of some classic literary works.' Ruggiero's thesis is that crime and crime control can be viewed through the lens of literature rather than the law and that the literary view draws attention to the significance of value, emotion, and the imagination in understanding crime and crime control. The book consists of ten chapters that address a particular criminological issue by means of either a particular literary work, a particular author, or a combination of authors and works. The phenomena analysed through the lens of literature are: atavism, organised crime, illegal drugs, gender, ethnicity, industrial crime, differential association, corruption, imprisonment, and state crime. A summary of the chapter on ethnicity provides a representative example of how Ruggiero employs literature to communicate sociological meaning and elaborate criminological analysis. He (Ruggiero 2003: 105) takes the following as his starting point: 'Ethnic minorities as a "problem" appear in criminological analysis as offenders and, to a lesser degree, as victims, generating debate around marginalization, violence, institutional racism and other related issues.' The problem of ethnicity in criminology – the problem of the marginalisation and racism to which ethnic minorities are subjected both in society and within the criminal justice system – is viewed through the lens of James Baldwin's (1964) play, *Blues for Mister Charlie*, and Richard Wright's (1940) novel, *Native Son*. *Blues for Mister Charlie* focuses on the all-pervasive character of racist exclusion in segregated societies, with racially motivated murder understood as merely an extreme version of this exclusion in these societies. Ruggiero argues that Baldwin was in fact communicating the concept of hate crime and elaborating its criminological significance decades before it was criminalised in the US. *Native Son* focuses on the relationship between being violated and perpetrating violence, exemplified in the protagonist, Bigger Thomas. Thomas is an African American man who murders a white woman and the trajectory of his life is concisely captured in the titles of the three parts of the novel: *Fear*, *Flight*, and *Fate*. Ruggiero argues that Wright makes a clear case for inequality as the cause of the crimes committed by Thomas and as a cause of violent crime more generally.

In his analysis of *Native Son*, Ruggiero mentions Wright's engagement with sociology and quotes from an introduction Wright wrote to St Clair Drake and Horace R. Cayton's (1945) *Black Metropolis: A Study of Negro Life in a Northern City*, a seminal anthropological and sociological study of Chicago's South Side. It is worth quoting from that introduction at greater length than Ruggiero:

> But let me bluntly warn the reader at the outset: This is no easy book. In order to understand it you may have to wrench your mind rather violently out of your accustomed ways of thinking. There is no attempt in *Black Metropolis* to understate, to gloss over, to doll up, or make harsh facts pleasant for the tender-minded. The facts of urban life presented here are in their starkest form, their crudest manifestation; not because the authors want to shock you, but because the environment out of which those facts spring has so wrought them. To have presented them otherwise would have been to negate the humanity of the American Negro (Wright 1945: ix).

This passage provides a perfect counterpoint to Ruggiero's interpretation of *Native Son* and draws attention to the need for a sociological imagination, for wrenching your mind rather violently out of your accustomed ways of thinking. Wright has deployed his own sociological imagination in *Native Son*, representing the consequences of the inequality documented in *Black Metropolis* in the personality and life experience of the novel's protagonist. This deployment of the imagination, by means of which meaning is communicated and concepts elaborated, is precisely what Ruggiero claims that literature can do for criminology, with Baldwin and Wright explaining the evaluative and emotional aspects of hate crime and structural inequality respectively. Although Ruggiero makes extensive and creative use of literary examples, his discussion of his research framework is limited and it is not entirely clear whether, for example, the communication and elaboration that literature can achieve is unique to literary works specifically, unique to fiction more generally, or could be achieved in other ways. I think an accurate characterisation of Ruggiero's thesis is that narrative fiction, documentaries, and discursive texts can all communicate sociological meaning and elaborate criminological analysis, but that literature specifically and fiction more generally are particularly proficient at wrenching readers' minds out of accustomed ways of thinking by means of the imagination.

Ruggiero's (2003) best-known analysis is the sixth chapter of the book, 'Moby Dick and the Crimes of the Economy', which was previously published as a journal article (Ruggiero 2002). Frauley (2010: 65) writes of this analysis: 'Ruggiero's work is exemplary: he does not simply assert or construct a normative value position but illustrates the value of fiction for criminology by constructing an [*sic*] criminological narrative of *Moby Dick* and a number of other works of classic fiction.' Where the cultural criminological framework cannot move beyond the text in virtue of its constructionism and restricts textual meaning to the intended meaning expressed by the author or director, Ruggiero's approach is 'broadly realist' (Frauley 2010: 52). Frauley identifies three elements in Ruggiero's realism: independence of meaning, authorisation, and the relationship between textual meaning and extratextual reality. The idea is that it is the text rather than the authorial or directorial intention that authorises meaning and that meaning is produced by the reader or audience within the constraints established by the text. In reading Herman Melville's (1851) *Moby-Dick; or, The Whale* I need not thus obsess about Melville's intentions, but nor am I free to interpret the novel in any way I want – for example, as an elaboration of the concept of patriotism in terms of the need for heroic self-sacrifice in the face of a threat to national sovereignty. In Frauley's (2010: 57) terms, 'texts "authorize" the meaning that is to be found in them. Hence, the text constrains our reading and disciplines our imagination; that is, the text authorizes what we can imagine as a plausible interpretation'. In literary texts, the language used determines the structure of the fictional world and this, in turn, determines textual meaning. The relationship between textual meaning and extratextual reality is then determined by a combination of: linguistic structure, the analytic languages (or discourses) of criminology or sociology, the practices of reading, and the extent to which the fiction is characterised by truth as well as invention.

It is worth noting that very little of this is explicitly stated by Ruggiero. *Crime in Literature* opens with a brief introduction that consists of the statement of intent I quoted previously, a short rationale, and an extended abstract. Ruggiero (2003: 235) furthermore has little to say about his methodology, makes no significant links among the literary analyses in the different chapters, and offers no conclusion to the monograph beyond a 'Post scriptum' of six lines. This is not a criticism of Ruggiero (I agree with most of Frauley's commendation of his work), but an indication that the critical realist framework which Frauley attributes to Ruggiero appears to at least some extent to have been retrospectively applied to *Crime in Literature*. For my purposes, the important point is that Frauley and Ruggiero share not only a realist approach to social reality, but a critical realist framework within that approach. While I am sympathetic to this framework, I cannot share it as – to use the literary critical terminology – I am more of an *intentionalist* than Frauley because I do not regard textual meaning as entirely independent of authorial or directorial intention (Lamarque 2009). With respect to literature, I have previously argued that literary language is not a medium with essential features that ground the property of literariness, but a literary use of language, an employment of language that is characterised by a match between authorial intention on the one hand and reader appreciation on the other hand (McGregor 2016). Following from my conception of fiction as a rule-bound practice (discussed in Chapter 1), I regard the meaning of the text as co-created by authorial intention and reader interpretation, both of which are constrained by the text itself. In consequence, my interpretation of *Moby-Dick* as a call for self-sacrificial patriotism must be based on the text if it is to convince. Similarly, the discovery of a letter by Melville making the same claim would only authorise the interpretation if it was supported in the text. Where the critical realist framework excludes all authorial intention, my framework includes authorial intention that is supported in the text. The difference is a subtle one, because this particular letter would be treated in the same way by both Frauley and I, but it is sufficient to preclude my adoption of the critical realist framework.

Frauley evaluates Ruggiero's contribution to establishing the relationship between narrative fiction and criminological inquiry in terms of two features. First, Ruggiero develops a realist approach to narrative fiction, which articulates both the independence of the text from authorial intention and the relationship between the fictional representation and reality. Frauley (2010: 66–67) recognises the complexity of the relation between fiction and truth and reads Ruggiero as having provided evidence for his preferred characterisation, by Garry Potter (1998): 'Ruggiero's study demonstrates Potter's argument that there is "truth in fiction" – that fiction is always connected to reality and that through fiction we can discern valuable knowledge about our social world'. Second, 'Ruggiero explicitly situates fiction as both a *pedagogical* and *analytic* tool' (Frauley 2010: 51). Literature has pedagogic value because it is a tool for communicating sociological meaning and analytic value because it is a tool for the elaboration of criminological analysis. My take on Ruggiero is that he does not surpass the pedagogic role of narrative fiction, but I shall make this case against the critical realist framework as a whole, after I have discussed Frauley's theory of fictional realities.

Frauley's critical realism

Frauley (2010: xi) begins *Criminology, Deviance, and the Silver Screen: The Fictional Reality and the Criminological Imagination* with both a clear statement of his aim and a disclaimer:

> This is not a book about film. It is about the usefulness of fictional realities for a craft practice of theorizing. It uses film as a vehicle for analytic reflection on criminological and sociological ideas and as a tool for illustrating these ideas. These ideas, these concepts, can and must be operated to extract criminological significance and meaning from social objects. In this sense, they are tools.

Frauley's thesis is sophisticated, arguing first for a greater recognition of the significance of theory and the practice of theorising within criminology and then for the value of fictional realities for theory and theorising. Frauley maintains that the fictional realities presented in literature and cinema both (1) exemplify concepts and theories and (2) provide empirical referents for concepts and theories. *Empirical referents* are 'the means by which we can explore criminological concepts and their value for conceptualizing broader features of sociality' (Frauley 2010: 17). Frauley's focus is, as his title suggests, on cinematic rather than literary fictions, a choice that seems to have been informed by his extensive use of film in his teaching practice (and perhaps also a desire to complement Ruggiero's work on literature). The book consists of two parts, the first of which addresses the concern about the recognition of theory in criminology and the second of which demonstrates the way in which particular films exemplify particular concepts and theories. The first part explains the significance of analytic languages, fictional social realities, and the criminological imagination. The second part consists of cinematic explorations of four theories: Jack Katz's (1988) moral transcendence; American and British approaches to subcultural theories of deviance; Peter Conrad and Joseph Schneider's (1980) medicalisation thesis; and Michel Foucault's (1961, 1975, 1976) biological politics of life.

Frauley (2010: 31) characterises the previous employment of fictional realities by criminologists (with the exception of Ruggiero) as follows: 'There is a precedent for the analytical and pedagogical use of "fictional realities" in criminology, but in general this has been limited to seeing fiction and film as a stock of readily accessible and useful examples rather than as complex objects to be deconstructed and theorized.' Frauley agrees that narrative fictions offer accessible and useful examples and illustrate or exemplify theory (pedagogic role), but clearly considers the deconstruction and theorisation of fictional realities as complex objects as surpassing this capacity. I began this chapter with a brief discussion of my own teaching practice and the pedagogic value I saw in *End of Watch*. For Frauley, films are (like literature for Ruggiero) both pedagogic and analytic tools. Frauley conceives of analytic value as an extension of pedagogic value (a relationship I discuss later) and it is helpful to consider the pedagogic and analytic values of cinematic fictions as a continuum. On the pedagogic end are: narrative fictions representing experience in a dramatic or captivating manner (my intended use for *End of Watch*), narrative fictions as tools for critical thinking (Rafter 2006), narrative fictions as communicating sociological or criminological meaning (Ruggiero 2003), and narrative fictions as illustrating or exemplifying criminological concepts or theories (Frauley 2010). Falling somewhere in between the pedagogic and analytic are analytic models of narrative fiction (Cavender and Jurik 2012) and the elaboration of criminological analysis (Ruggiero 2003). Of the uses discussed thus far, this leaves only narrative fiction as an empirical referent for criminological theory (Frauley 2010) on the analytic end. Frauley's (2010) most detailed description of the analytic value of film appears in Chapter Four of his book, in his interpretation of Joel Schumacher's *Falling Down* (1993), which also constitutes his most detailed cinematic interpretation.

Frauley (2010: 114) differentiates between cinematic fiction illustrating theory and cinematic fiction as an empirical referent as follows:

> The film, *Falling Down*, can be theorized as a protracted effort to illustrate the process of symbolic transformation in which Bill Foster participates. This is not something that simply happens to Bill; it is something that is actively constructed by Bill through the intersection of social and cognitive processes. Paying attention to process in *Falling Down* and treating the film as an empirical referent to which Katz's concepts can be applied helps us to examine and clarify Katz's theoretical position and particular mode of theorizing, just as Katz's theoretical concepts can help us examine *Falling Down*.

On the pedagogic side, the film illustrates Katz's (1988) theory of moral transcendence. This is similar to my intended use of *End of Watch* except that while I was concerned with police practice, Frauley is concerned with criminological theory. *Falling Down* not only illustrates Katz's theory, however, but provides a protracted illustration in which his conceptions of line of interpretation, emotional process, and path of action shape the protagonist's emergent criminality and in which his conceptions of omens, spells and incantations, sacrificial violence, Godly judgement, and idolatry shape the experience of the cinematic narrative for the audience. The illustration is complex, occurring simultaneously on several levels, and creates a reciprocal relationship between the cinematic fiction and Katz's criminology. Frauley describes this relationship in terms of Katz's concepts being embedded in the fictional reality to the extent that the film exemplifies concept and theory in textured detail and his interpretation of the film enhances the cinematic experience by revealing deeper and more nuanced elements of the form and content of the fictional narrative. The difference between exemplifying criminological theories and providing empirical referents for criminological theories is thus one of degree rather than kind. Cinematic fictions are classified as empirical referents for (rather than mere illustrations of) theories in virtue of the extent to which the concepts and arguments of the theory are embedded in the fictional reality. This is true of not just cinematic fictions in Frauley, but literary fictions in Ruggiero, that is of the critical realist framework in general.

I hope to have made my admiration for Frauley's (2010) achievement in *Criminology, Deviance, and the Silver Screen* clear. The book deserves a much wider readership and would, were more criminologists in agreement with Frauley as to the significance of the criminological imagination, have had a much greater impact within the discipline. I have for the most part followed Frauley in his analyses of the cultural criminological framework, Rafter, and Ruggiero and found very little with which to disagree. I am also sympathetic to the critical realist framework he establishes for his own and Ruggiero's theoretical contributions to the discipline. Notwithstanding, all of the functions of narrative fiction in the Ruggiero-Frauley framework are variations on the pedagogic role. Frauley's most detailed discussion of the use of film as an analytic tool conceives of the fictional reality as an empirical referent in terms of protracted illustration; that is, as an extension of the use of film as an accessible example, instance, or illustration of theory or practice. As such, the pedagogic and analytic values of narrative fiction articulated by Ruggiero and Frauley are more accurately characterised as a continuum than a dichotomy. In this continuum, narrative fictions perform the pedagogic role of facilitating, augmenting, or enhancing the communication of knowledge, from their most basic use in representing lived experience (my intention for *End of Watch*) to providing a sophisticated and nuanced empirical referent for a criminological theory (Frauley's use for *Falling Down*). These uses range from the descriptive (mine) to the analytic (Frauley's), but are all realisations of pedagogic value, concerned with the way in which criminological knowledge is communicated rather than providing knowledge of the causes of crime and social harm.

There is only one place in *Criminology, Deviance, and the Silver Screen* where Frauley (2010: 73) gestures towards the aetiological role – where, in the context of introducing the criminological imagination, he describes analytic languages as extracting criminological insight from 'nontraditional sources of data'. My interest in narrative fiction is precisely in this, in literary or cinematic works as fulfilling the aetiological role by providing a source of data about the causes of crime and social harm. *Case study* is an abbreviation of case-based research, a research design in which a single case is studied intensively for the purpose of understanding a population. Case studies are usually used for the purposes of developing rather than testing theory (Perri 6 and Bellamy 2011). The term is also used more loosely, to describe the illustration of practice or theory by means of an example (my use in the introduction to this chapter), but my claim is that narrative fiction can be employed as a case study in the former sense; that is, as a source of data about the causes of crime and social harm. In the remainder of this book, I employ seven case studies in support of my argument.

Narrative justice

In *Narrative Justice* (McGregor 2018b) I defend the thesis that criminal inhumanity can be reduced by the cultivation of narrative sensibility. *Narrative sensibility* can be understood as the awareness of narrative values and sensitivity to the ways in which cognitive, ethical, and political values are realised in and attributed to narrative representations. The idea is that an individual who experiences, researches, or produces narratives becomes more sensitive to the form of narratives, the content of narratives, and the interaction of form and content in ways that are cognitively, ethically, and politically valuable. *Criminal inhumanity* is the term I employ to denote serious crimes committed by a state or non-state actor against a government, public, or civilian population for ideological reasons. I use *ideology* to denote a systematic scheme of ideas or set of beliefs that govern conduct rather than the more specific Marxist denotation as the means by which the most powerful class maintains the dominance of their own ideas or beliefs in society (Marx and Engels 1846; Rafter 2006). Criminal inhumanity is a category of crime that is justified by ethical principles, which provide the foundation for ideological motivation. Narrative justice is an instantiation of aesthetic education, the thesis that there is a tripartite relationship among the aesthetic, ethical, and political spheres of value such that the cultivation of aesthetic sensibility develops political harmony (Schiller 1794).

The first six chapters of *Narrative Justice* are theoretical, arguing for the proposed relation between narrative sensibility and criminal inhumanity and addressing objections from literary theory and philosophy. The narrative justice thesis is underpinned by the theory of narrative ethical knowledge, which holds that exemplary narratives convey phenomenological ethical knowledge in virtue of their narrativity. *Phenomenological ethical knowledge* is the realisation of what a particular lived ethical experience is like. There is thus a causal relation between the adoption of the preferred set of cognitive, emotional, and evaluative responses of an exemplary narrative and the acquisition of phenomenological ethical knowledge. This ethical development does not refer to either the behaviour of an audience member or to their moral character, but simply to their increased understanding. The argument then proceeds as follows: if (1) the cultivation of narrative sensibility can develop ethical understanding and (2) criminal inhumanity is a category of crime that is justified by ethical principles, then (3) the cultivation of narrative sensibility has the potential to reduce criminal inhumanity. The jump from (1) and (2) to (3) is made in consequence of the well-established relation in criminology between theoretical explanation of the causes of crime and the reduction of crime in practice. This argument formulates narrative justice as a thesis of aesthetic education by elevating the link between narrative representation and the ethical sphere in narrative ethical knowledge to the political sphere. In this respect, it is a development of both J.C. Friedrich von Schiller's (1794) original thesis and two recent contributions to the tradition: Gayatri Chakravorty Spivak's (2012) poststructuralist argument for the relevance of the literary imagination to political harmony and Sarah Worth's (2017) neo-Aristotelian argument for the relevance of narrative understanding to social harmony.

The final three chapters of *Narrative Justice* are practical, applying the thesis to concrete examples. These examples demonstrate how exemplary narratives can reduce ideologically-motivated crime by: evaluating responsibility for inhumanity, answering the specific question of what, if anything, the posthumous accusations of collaboration with the Third Reich revealed celebrated literary theorist Paul de Man to have done wrong; affording an understanding of the psychology of inhumanity, solving the evaluative problem of the apparent conflict of aesthetic and ethical value as instantiated in the narrative representation of torturers in South Africa under apartheid; and undermining extremist recruitment strategies, identifying white supremacist and Muslim fundamentalist conceptions of victimhood as identical. In each case, the explanation of criminal inhumanity is achieved by a comparative analysis of two exemplary narratives, either one documentary and one fictional (evaluating responsibility and understanding psychology) or both documentary (undermining recruitment). The practical applications of the thesis locate it within the narrative criminological framework. I make this claim on the basis of the following commitments of narrative justice: stories are a significant explanatory variable in criminology, stories are relevant to the causes of crime and social harm, stories are relevant to desistance from crime and social harm, realism is preferable to positivism and constructionism, narrative form is criminologically significant, and the relationship between narrative and ethics is criminologically significant. There are only two points of divergence with Presser (2008, 2013, 2018). Where she conceives of narratives as constitutive and is concerned with nonfiction narratives alone, I conceive of narratives as representational and am concerned with both nonfictional and fictional narratives. There is a closer match between my narrative justice thesis and the narrative criminological framework than between my criminology of narrative fiction and the narrative criminological framework and the most accurate way to describe the respective relationships is my previous work as *located within* and my current work as *emergent from* that framework (as discussed in Chapter 2).

I conclude *Narrative Justice* by suggesting that I may have established a new methodology for criminological inquiry. Subsequently, in my introduction to a symposium on the book, I (McGregor 2020a) argue for narrative justice as a methodology on the grounds of cohesion among the theories, principles, and methods developed: the theories of the ethical and cognitive values of exemplary narratives determine the principle of phenomenological ethical knowledge which, in combination with the principle of the crime reduction potential of causal explanation, underpins the methods of disclosure (the comparative analysis of a documentary and a fiction) and demystification (the comparative analysis of two documentaries). Whether or not narrative justice succeeds as a criminological methodology, it does not — and was not intended to — provide evidence for the aetiological role of narrative fiction.[3] Narrative justice is exclusively concerned with fictional narratives as they stand in relation to documentaries, with the capacity of narrative fictions to supplement the knowledge conveyed by documentaries. There is no implication that narrative fictions can provide data independently of documentaries or that fictions could be treated as case studies. I mention my argument for narrative justice as a methodology partly for the purpose of further distinguishing my current and previous criminological engagements with fiction, but also to suggest another way of conceiving of Frauley's (2010) contribution to the discipline. Frauley's meticulous and comprehensive discussion of analytic languages, fictional social realities, and the criminological imagination in *Criminology, Deviance, and the Silver Screen* establishes both a critical realist framework for his and Ruggerio's research and a methodology within that framework. This provides additional evidence for my claim that Frauley's work is deserving of wider recognition, but does not alter my claim that the Ruggiero-Frauley framework is restricted to the pedagogic role of narrative fiction in criminological inquiry.

Conclusion

Where the previous chapter positioned my criminology of narrative fiction as emergent from the narrative criminological framework, this chapter has positioned my contribution in relation to current criminological engagements with narrative fiction. I began by identifying three epistemic roles for narrative fiction in criminological inquiry: semiotic, pedagogic, and aetiological. With these roles in mind, I addressed the three most substantial engagements with narrative fiction in criminology to date: the cultural criminological framework, the critical realist framework, and my own work in *Narrative Justice* (McGregor 2018b). I addressed each of the engagements in terms of the roles, taking my lead from Frauley (2010) in examining cultural criminology, Rafter's (2006) theory of crime films, and Ruggiero's (2003) criminological analyses of literature. I argued first that Rafter's theory of crime films is most accurately located within the cultural criminological framework and second that the cultural criminological framework cannot provide knowledge of the reality beyond the representation in consequence of being underpinned by a constructionist approach to social reality. As such, cultural criminology is restricted to treating fictional narrative as either providing knowledge of the production and reception of representations of crime and its control (semiotic role) or as facilitating, augmenting, or enhancing the communication of criminological knowledge (pedagogic role).

I then turned to the critical realist framework, within which both Ruggerio's criminological analyses of literature and Frauley's theory of fictional realities are located. The critical realist framework establishes the following relationship between representation and reality: the language (in literature) or combination of language and imagery (in cinema) determines the structure of the fictional world, which in turn determines the textual (literary or cinematic) meaning; the relationship between textual meaning and extratextual reality is then determined by the combination of linguistic (literary) or linguistic and pictorial (cinematic) structure, the analytic languages (discourses) of criminology or sociology, the practices of reading (literature) or viewing (cinema), and the extent to which fiction is characterised by truth as well as invention. Ruggiero and Frauley both work within this framework and both develop theories of the pedagogic and analytic values of literature (Ruggiero) and cinema (Frauley). I claimed that despite the various characterisations of narrative fictions as analytic tools – in terms of elaborating criminological analysis and providing an empirical referent for criminological theory – both Ruggiero and Frauley in fact restrict narrative fiction to a pedagogic role in criminological inquiry. The extent and sophistication of narrative fiction as a pedagogic tool varies greatly, from my simple example of *End of Watch* illustrating the realities of policing hard to reach communities to Frauley's complex example of *Falling Down* providing an empirical referent for Katz's moral transcendence. All such examples nonetheless employ narrative fiction as an illustration, facilitating the communication of knowledge of a practice, concept, or theory rather than providing knowledge of the causes of crime or social harm.

Finally, I considered my previous work within the narrative criminological framework. Narrative justice is the thesis that narrative sensibility can reduce criminal inhumanity and, as such, is also part of the tradition of aesthetic education in philosophy, which articulates a tripartite relationship among the aesthetic, ethical, and political spheres of value.

After summarising the thesis and its practical applications, I referred to my argument for narrative justice as a criminological methodology, combining theories and principles with a method involving the comparative analysis of documentary and fictional narratives for the purposes of either disclosure or demystification (McGregor 2020a). I concluded that while both my thesis and the Ruggiero-Frauley framework articulated a methodology for criminological inquiry, neither employed narrative fictions in the aetiological role in which I am interested. The purpose of my criminology of narrative fiction is to argue that fictional narratives can be used as case studies, as sources of data about the causes of crime and social harm. I contend that there are at least three types of knowledge that narrative fiction can provide – phenomenological, counterfactual, and mimetic – and that these types of knowledge are criminological, that is can explain the causes of crime and social harm. My argument begins in the next chapter, where I demonstrate that narrative fiction can provide phenomenological knowledge of the causes of crime and social harm.

4

Phenomenological Criminology

Introduction

James Mangold's *Cop Land* (1997) is set in New York and New Jersey in the nineteen seventies. A group of corrupt New York Police Department (NYPD) officers, led by Lieutenant Ray Donlan (played by Harvey Keitel), have taken advantage of a loophole in police regulations to establish a community with their families outside the city, in the tiny town of Garrison, New Jersey. They have orchestrated the appointment of a local hero, Freddy Heflin (played by Sylvester Stallone), as sheriff for the dual purpose of keeping the peace and turning a blind eye to the police officers' links to organised crime. Heflin saved Liz Randone (played Annabella Sciorra) from drowning in his youth, suffering permanent damage to his hearing in consequence of which he was unable to realise his dream of joining the NYPD. He is treated as a second-class citizen by the police residents of Garrison, a hierarchy he does not challenge, apparently content with his comfortable but largely ineffectual role. The plot of the film revolves around Donlan's plan to murder his own nephew, Officer Murray Babitch (played by Michael Rapaport), to cover up two incidents of police misconduct. Donlan is already under investigation by the NYPD's Internal Affairs Bureau (IAB) and Heflin is asked for help in building a case against him by Lieutenant Moe Tilden (played by Robert De Niro):

> And besides the church traffic and the cats in the trees and all that other ... bullshit, okay ... there isn't much here for you to do, to keep your mind busy. But I look at you, Sheriff, and I see a man who's waiting for something to do ... and, here I am, here I am saying, Sheriff, I got something for you to do. (*Cop Land* 1997)

Heflin fails to act. He is then approached by Babitch, who is on the run from his colleagues following the murder of another police officer by Donlan. Again, he fails to act. By the time he makes the belated decision to provide Tilden with evidence in order to save Babitch's life, Donlan has already made use of his high-ranking police and municipal associates to close the IAB investigation down. In quick succession, Heflin is abandoned by Tilden, by Liz, by his only friend in the NYPD, and by both of his deputies. Heflin reflects that his single act of self-sacrifice cost him his hearing and limited his career prospects to what Tilden describes as being "the sheriff of cop land" (*Cop Land* 1997). Heflin also recognises that an attempt to save Babitch on his own is likely to cost him his life. The field of reasons for inaction is thus compelling, but he becomes increasingly disgusted with the choices he has made since saving Liz and with the way he has been manipulated by Donlan. He realises the lack of worth in the life he has been living and finds the moral and physical courage to take action, arresting Babitch, running the gauntlet of Donlan's coterie, and delivering Babitch safely to Tilden. What Mangold achieves by shaping Heflin's story into the form it takes in the film is to provide the audience with knowledge of what a particular lived experience is like, specifically the lived experience of being a law enforcement officer who facilitates – and, in so doing, participates in – police corruption.

Following my introduction to criminology, narrative representation, and fiction in Chapter 1, Chapters 2 and 3 constituted an extended literature review, locating my inquiry with respect to first the narrative criminological framework and then the cultural criminological and critical realist frameworks. My conclusion at the end of Chapter 3 was that, while my framework shared characteristics of both narrative criminology and critical realism, it was most accurately situated as emergent from the narrative criminological framework – although classification in terms of previous research is not essential to my criminology of narrative fiction. My argument for that criminology begins in this chapter. The argument moves beyond the previous criminological engagements with fiction to demonstrate the aetiological role of fiction; that is, fiction as a source of data about the causes of crime and social harm. The aetiological claim is based on the phenomenological, counterfactual, and mimetic values of narrative fictions. These values are, in turn, a function of the phenomenological, counterfactual, and mimetic knowledge that narrative fictions can provide. My claim is thus that some narrative fictions are sources of data about the causes of crime and social harm in virtue of providing knowledge of what certain experiences are like, knowledge of possible but non-existent situations, and detailed and accurate knowledge of everyday reality. Narrative fictions most often provide two or even all three of these types of knowledge simultaneously, but for the purposes of constructing my argument I shall focus on each in isolation, beginning with phenomenological knowledge in this chapter.

Recall from Chapter 1 that the relation between fictional people, places, and events in fictional representations and the world is understood in terms of reference to universals, to types of people, places, and events in the world rather than particular people, places, and events in the world. I used the examples of *The Godfather* (1972) and *Queen of the South (season 1)* (2016) by way of explanation. *The Godfather* refers to the type of person that accepts his criminal inheritance and the knowledge provided by the narrative fiction is about both Michael Corleone (in the fictional reality) and types of people like him (in the real world). Similarly, *Queen of the South* refers to the close relationship between victimisation and offending in the experience of criminalised women and the knowledge provided by the narrative fiction is about both Teresa Mendoza[1] (in the fictional reality) and types of people like her (in the real world). If the knowledge provided by narrative fictions – whether phenomenological, counterfactual, or mimetic – did not extend beyond the narrative representations, then it would be very difficult, if not impossible, to argue for the criminological value or values of those fictions. My argument for those values involves the use of detailed case studies to demonstrate the way in which narrative fictions provide phenomenological, counterfactual, and mimetic knowledge respectively.

This chapter proceeds with an explanation of phenomenological knowledge in terms of its relation to the narrative framework characteristic of exemplary narratives, that is the preferred set (or sets) of cognitive, evaluative, and emotional responses to the representation produced by its opacity. I refine my concern with the phenomenological knowledge conveyed by narrative frameworks to phenomenological knowledge of the perpetrators of crime or social harm, on the basis of the aetiological value of this knowledge. I then explore the phenomenological value of two narrative fictions by the use of two case studies, each of which demonstrates a particular way in which narrative fictions provide phenomenological knowledge. Martin Amis' (2014) novel, *The Zone of Interest*, provides knowledge of what it is like to conspire in genocide by representing the lived experience of the perpetrators of the National Socialist genocide during the Second World War, suggesting a parallel between Auschwitz and the Guantanamo Bay detention camp (GTMO). Tom King and Mitch Gerads' (2018) graphic novel, *The Sheriff of Babylon*, provides knowledge of what it is like to collaborate in a military occupation by representing the lived experience of a contractor for the Coalition Provisional Authority in Iraq, suggesting that all such collaboration contributes to mass harm. Both the novel and the graphic novel reveal motivations of perpetrators of crime and social harm that would not be feasible for nonfictional representations. My conclusion is that in providing phenomenological knowledge of the lived experience of the fictional offenders, the case studies provide explanations of the causes of actual crime and social harm, data that could be employed in the reduction or prevention of those crimes and social harms.

Phenomenological knowledge

Dorothy Walsh (1969: 96) employs Gilbert Ryle's (1949) *The Concept of Mind* to delineate two distinct types of knowledge:

> A philosophical analysis of the meaning of 'know' that is at present widely influential is one that finds two fundamental and irreducible meanings in use. There is knowing in the sense of *knowing that* (such and such is so) and there is knowing in the sense of *knowing how* (to perform some act).

She (Walsh 1969: 103) then differentiates between experience as *awareness of* and experience as *living through* and advances the latter as a third type of knowledge:

> *Recognizing* that such and such is so with reference to some kind of human experience is not the same as *realizing* what this might be like as a lived experience. Confession of failure to understand, in the sense of realize, is perfectly compatible with absence of doubt concerning matter-of-fact.

Catherine Wilson (1983: 492) refers to this realisation as 'knowing what', short for 'knowing-what-it-is-like', and John Gibson (2008: 582) as 'experiential knowledge'. Walsh claims that unlike actual experiences, the virtual experiences of literary works can be experienced by anyone who engages with the work such that they are shareable and can provide knowledge. Alex Burri (2007: 310) holds a similar view, maintaining that the practice of art aims at the subjective rather than objective representation of reality, 'to conduct some kind of *phenomenological investigation* into how things appear to us'. Walsh thus identifies three distinct types of knowledge that representations can provide: knowledge-that (such and such is so), knowledge-how (to perform some act), and knowledge-what (something is like). My focus in this chapter is exclusively on knowledge-what. In their introductory text, Stephan Käufer and Anthony Chemero (2015) describe phenomenology as having two primary concerns, with the structures that make a shared, objective world intelligible to human beings and with describing subjective human experience in detail. I am concerned with the latter, with the subjective rather than objective representation of reality, specifically with the subjective representation of reality in narrative fictions. In consequence, *phenomenological knowledge* is knowledge of what a particular lived experience is like.

Recall from Chapter 1 that the difference between exemplary narratives and minimal narratives – the combination of causal relations, thematic unity, and closure – is that the latter are *opaque*, meaning that their authors or directors provide a particular perspective on the characters, settings, and actions represented by means of this combination. The perspective that constitutes an exemplary narrative produces a *framework*, which is a preferred set (or sets) of cognitive, evaluative, and emotional responses to the narrative, such that the reader or member of the audience is invited to adopt particular emotional responses and evaluative attitudes to the characters, settings, and actions. Gregory Currie (2010) notes that there are no explicit instructions, but that the framework is expressed by the way in which the sequence of events is represented in the narrative. From this framework Currie (2010: 106) proceeds to

> the *standard mode of engagement* with narrative. Narratives, because they serve as expressive of the points of view of their narrators, create in our minds the image of a persona with that point of view, thereby prompting us to imitate salient aspects of it –notably evaluative attitudes and emotional responses. In taking on those responses, we thereby come to adopt, wholly or in part, the framework canonical for that work.

The standard mode of engagement is thus the adoption, by readers or audiences, of the framework that the author or director invites one to adopt. It is this framework – the preferred set of cognitive, evaluative, and emotional responses – that has the capacity to provide phenomenological knowledge. Authors and directors can provide different frameworks on the same (or similar) characters, settings, and actions. In *The Siege* (1998), Edward Zwick frames the torture of suspected terrorists as unacceptable, even in a case where the suspect is believed to possess information that could save lives, in virtue of the fact that its employment undermines the very principles that underpin the US constitution. The resort to torture is consequently represented as an admission of defeat. In contrast, Kathryn Bigelow frames the torture of suspected terrorists as justified by its goal, the locating and killing of Osama bin Laden, in *Zero Dark Thirty* (2012). Bigelow represents torture as a regrettable but nonetheless necessary means whose moral and practical disadvantages are outweighed by the reason for its use, victory in the War on Terror.

Gibson (2008: 582–583) explains how art provides phenomenological knowledge, using a novel and a film (both fictional narratives) as examples:

> Drawing solely on my own experiences and my preferred books of theory, I will acquire no significant knowledge of what it is like to be a victim of systematic racial oppression or an immigrant struggling to make his way to an unwelcoming country. But I can read Ralph Ellison's *Invisible Man* or watch Elia Kazan's *America, America* [*sic*] and in so doing acquaint myself with a region of human experience that would otherwise remain unknown to me.

Importantly, this phenomenological knowledge is, given the relationship between fiction and reality mentioned in the previous section, knowledge of the actual lived experience of the types of people to which the works refer rather than just knowledge of the lived experience of the fictional characters. In order to acquire the phenomenological knowledge, it is necessary not just to experience the respective representations, but to accept the author or director's invitation to adopt an approved set of cognitive, evaluative, and emotional responses to experience the representation in a particular way. For example, if one fails to accept Ellison's invitation to regard the anonymous narrator of *Invisible Man* as a sympathetic character, then one will not realise what it is like to be a victim of systematic racial oppression and will not acquire the relevant phenomenological knowledge. In *Zero Dark Thirty*, Bigelow represents the torture of Ammar al-Baluchi (played by Reda Kateb) from the point of view of a witness to the torture (Maya, played by Jessica Chastain). Members of the audience that adopt the standard mode of engagement to the cinematic representation are provided with the knowledge of what it is like to witness the Central Intelligence Agency's (CIA) enhanced interrogation. Many contemporary viewers may, however, reject the framing of Maya's complicity in crimes against humanity as justified by their end, in which case they will not acquire the knowledge-what, although one may well acquire knowledge-that (for example, the CIA used enhanced interrogation in the hunt for bin Laden) or knowledge-how (for example, enhanced interrogation is conducted). Viewers who do adopt Bigelow's framework do not have to become temporary or permanent enthusiasts for the War on Terror, but they must temporarily set aside their reservations about the CIA's official use of torture if they are to understand the lived experience of a participant in that war as represented in the film.

Criminological interest in lived experience is widespread, extending from the victims of crime or social harm to criminal justice workers and offenders (Presser 2009). My focus here is on the lived experience of the perpetrators of crime and social harm in virtue of the more direct link between their experiences and the criminological project. As noted in Chapter 1, I take the aim of the criminological project to be the reduction of crime or social harm, which is achieved by employing theoretical and empirical investigation and verification to direct or inform public policy and evidence-based practice. The key factor that links criminological research to crime or social harm reduction is the explanation of the cause of the crime or social harm. Phenomenological knowledge of the perpetrator of crime or social harm is more likely to explain the cause of that crime or social harm than phenomenological knowledge of the victims or criminal justice workers involved. In consequence, for my purposes, the *phenomenological value* of a representation is the extent to which that representation provides knowledge of the lived experience of perpetrating crime or social harm.

In Chapter 1 I distinguished between fictional and nonfictional representations on the basis of their production and reception within practices characterised by a tolerance for inventiveness, imaginativeness, and fabrication in fiction and a close correspondence between representation and reality in nonfiction. There is no necessary relation between fiction and falsity, imagination, or invention, however, in consequence of which there is no decisive reason that fictional representation should not be as valuable as nonfictional representations with respect to representing the lived experience of perpetrating crime or social harm. Some narrative fictions will have greater phenomenological value than some narrative nonfictions, providing more knowledge of what it is like to perpetrate certain crimes or social harms. There is also a sense in which fictional representations can provide phenomenological knowledge that is not available to nonfictional representations. Joshua Page and Philip Goodman (2018) discuss the difficulties of practising what Loïc Wacquant (2005) calls *carnal sociology* in the context of researching crime and punishment.

They note the problems of access and ethics with regard to experiencing or witnessing the embodied nature of behaviour in the environments in which criminologists are interested. In the case with which Page and Goodman are concerned, the embodiment of prisonisation, there are also legal considerations and they argue that Edward Bunker's (1977, 1981) fictionalised autobiographies can be employed to overcome these impediments to criminological analysis. Although he is referring to his study of the emotional and evaluative aspects of a boxing gym in *Body and Soul: Notebooks of an Apprentice Boxer* (Wacquant 2000), Wacquant (2005: 469) makes a comment that addresses doubts about the features characteristic of the practice of fiction:

> I hold that a concern for rhetorical composition and authority need not entail an abandonment of conceptual rigor and scientific veracity – in short, that 'blurred genres' of writing can serve the aims of a postpositivist social *science* rather than imply a wholesale surrender to the seductions of humanistic musing.

Extrapolating from the blurring of genres in Wacquant's autoethnography, inventiveness, imaginativeness, and fabrication are not necessarily incompatible with rigour and veracity and do not necessarily require the researcher to give up criminology for literary criticism. The ability of fictional representations to provide phenomenological and other knowledge that is unavailable to nonfictional representations for access, ethical, or legal reasons is an important component of the criminological value of fiction.

The Zone of Interest

Amis' (2014) novel, *The Zone of Interest*, is a paradigmatic example of a work of fiction that provides knowledge of the lived experience of perpetrating state crime, specifically the National Socialist genocide of Jews, Jehovah's Witnesses, Roma, Eastern Europeans, the disabled, homosexuals, and socialists in 1939–45.[2] The novel consists of six titled chapters, an Aftermath, and an Acknowledgments and Afterword. Each of the chapters is divided into three subtitled parts, narrated in the first person by one of the three protagonists: Angelus Thomsen, Paul Doll, and Szmul (given name never revealed). Thomsen is a mid-level bureaucrat who is the nephew of Martin Bormann, the *Reichsleiter* (head of the Nazi party), a genetic association that provides him with far more privilege than his honorary *Schutzstaffel* (SS) rank.

Doll is a concentration camp commandant, the SS officer in charge of extermination. Szmul is Doll's *Sonderkommandofuhrer*, a Jewish inmate in charge of a squad of inmates who prepare the new arrivals for the gas chambers and (attempt to) dispose of their bodies afterwards. The Aftermath is narrated by Thomsen, who is the most significant of the protagonists and the only one to survive the war with his sanity intact. The Acknowledgements and Afterword is by Amis, addressing readers directly and in his own voice.

The novel takes its title from the SS *interest zone*, a fifteen square mile area around the town of Auschwitz in the General Government of occupied Poland (Wachsmann 2015). The zone was cleared of inhabitants in 1940 and developed into a purpose-built complex of extermination, concentration, labour, and prisoner of war camps; armaments and chemical factories; barracks with accommodation for families; and agricultural stations to feed the garrison. The main camps were Auschwitz I (a concentration camp, *Kat Zet I* in the novel), Auschwitz II-Birkenau (an extermination camp, *Kat Zet II*), and Auschwitz III-Monowitz (a labour camp, *Kat Zet III*). The novel opens in Kat Zet I in August 1942 and the central narrative concludes at the end of April 1943, with the Aftermath (and novel) finishing in 1948. At this conclusion, Thomsen reflects on the *real* zone of interest, developing a point first mentioned by Szmul. Members of the *Sonderkommando* are themselves selected for extermination relatively quickly, but Szmul has survived longer than all of his subordinates in consequence of Doll's patronage. He writes:

> Once upon a time there was a king, and the king commissioned his favourite wizard to create a magic mirror. This mirror didn't show your reflection. It showed your soul – it showed who you really were. ... I find that the KZ is that mirror. The KZ is that mirror, but with only one difference. You can't turn away. (Amis 2014: 33)

Thomsen extends the kind of moral suicide to which Szmul refers to not just the outright collaboration of which he and Szmul are guilty, but to life in the Third Reich as a whole: 'Under National Socialism you looked in the mirror and saw your soul. You found yourself out. ... We all discovered, or helplessly revealed, who we were. Who somebody really was. *That* was the zone of interest' (Amis 2014: 285).

There are three literary devices employed by Amis that are of particular interest with respect to the phenomenological value of the novel. The first is the combination of narrators (the three protagonists) and narration (the use of the first person). The narration allows the reader to gain direct access to the thoughts of the three perpetrators of genocide, an access that would not be possible in nonfiction. Even if a perpetrator was interviewed, their thoughts would be mediated by their speech and the reader could never be sure that the perpetrator was being completely honest (especially when one considers the legal consequences of documented confession). In contrast, Thomsen and Szmul are quickly established as reliable narrators, well aware of their own failings and with the courage to confront them. Doll's narration is immediately established as unreliable in virtue of his fragile hold on his sanity. The first section that he narrates, 'The Selektion', reveals a pathological obsession with numbers, a pronounced lack of self-awareness, and a craving to be regarded as normal. Szmul considers the relationship between genocide perpetration and madness with greater insight:

> 'Either you go mad in the first ten minutes,' it is often said, 'or you get used to it.' You could argue that those who get used to it do in fact go mad. And there is another possible outcome: you don't go mad and you don't get used to it. (Amis 2014: 77)

The transparent access to the thoughts of Thomsen and Szmul and the opaque access to those of Doll, represented as a singular synthesis of self-deception and lucidity, provides psychological insight into the motivation, morality, and mental health of all three collaborators in genocide.

The second device extends beyond the explanation of the causes of collaboration in the individual perpetrators to the construction of an overarching pattern of meaning by the juxtaposition of the three narrators. All three are active participants in the genocide: Doll is the commandant of Kat Zet I and Kat Zet II (III has not been built at the time the novel opens); Szmul is responsible for the disposal of the corpses, which is problematic in consequence of the industrial scale on which they are being produced; and Thomsen is an official in the *Buna-Werke*, the IG Farben rubber factory that literally works slave labourers to death (even to the extent of inefficiency). Doll is a completely despicable character, a physical and moral coward who fantasises about physically and sexually abusing his wife, Hannah, but fears she will get the better of him in a fight. He is an enthusiastic perpetrator of genocide whose emotions do not extend beyond his own suffering (pressure to dispose of ever more corpses and a wife who refuses to perform marital duties) and is fully committed to the

Nazi cause. Szmul joined the Sonderkommando for several reasons, only one of which is selfish: to prolong his life, to exact revenge on the Nazis by recording their crimes (the sections of the novel narrated by him constitute a memoir he is writing), to make the inevitable deaths of those selected for extermination as painless as possible, and to use his knowledge of the process of selection to save lives in the few opportunities available. Szmul is unquestionably a victim of the genocide, his collaboration sustained by the combination of helplessness and hopefulness.

Thomsen is situated somewhere between Szmul and Doll, a cynical collaborator who is fully cognisant of the moral horror of the Nazis, but concerned for the most part with himself, his main interest being the serial seduction of as many women as possible. It is Thomsen's libido that initiates the central plot of the novel, which is essentially a love story. His initial interest in Hannah Doll is purely carnal: 'This would be a *big* fuck' (Amis 2014: 14). Ironically, Thomsen's relationship with her remains chaste throughout, evolving from unrequited lust to a deep, meaningful, and persistent love in which he places himself at risk to help her for no reward during the war and devotes a substantial amount of his resources to finding her following its conclusion. When he meets Hannah after three years of searching, he asks only for permission to correspond and maintain a long-distance friendship. As the novel progresses, Thomsen reveals that he has committed minor acts of sabotage at the rubber factory (rubber is essential to the war effort). His character appears to develop from almost complete selfishness to a growing concern for other people, a trajectory for which Hannah is a catalyst. Unlike Doll and despite his collaboration in genocide, Thomsen is not irredeemable and it is significant that the instrument of his redemption is Doll's wife.

The third literary device that is relevant to the phenomenological value of the novel is both more subtle and more complex than the first two. The way in which Amis represents the fictional reality of the narrative is faithful to the subjective experience of his three narrators, adhering closely to their respective points of view in each section of each chapter. Thomsen, Doll, and Szmul focus only on that which is important to them personally and exclude details that would assist readers in comprehending the specifics of the setting (details that are so familiar to the narrators that they do not require articulation). Thomsen initially identifies his location as only 'Kat Zet I' (Amis 2014: 1) and Doll his official role as extending 'Protective Custody' (Amis 2014: 20) to 50,000 people. The combination of this claustrophobically close first-person narration with a title that lacks an obvious context and the absence of a preamble of any sort infuses the novel with an atmosphere of vagueness. This is exacerbated by Amis' use of English translations for many (but not all) of the German names and terminology that is not associated with Auschwitz in the popular imagination. Examples of the latter include: the 'Equestrian Academy' (Amis 2014: 1), 'figures in city business suits' (Amis 2014: 88), 'Summer Huts' (Amis 2014: 96), and 'St Andrew's in the Old Town' (Amis 2014: 129). The vague atmosphere draws attention to the referential relation between fiction and reality that I noted earlier, in which the subject of the novel is not just Auschwitz in particular, but concentration camps in general, an international institution whose use can be traced at least as far back as 1900, by the British Empire during the Second Boer War (Kruger 1959).

Amis achieves more than drawing attention to the reference to universals characteristic of fiction, however, hinting at the contemporary relevance of the novel by means of incongruous reminders of America. These are sparse, but conspicuous: a part of the zone is called 'Kalifornia' (Amis 2014: 39); 'both [of Thomsen's] parents, in 1929, died in an elevator plunge in New York' (Amis 2014: 72); and Thomsen's use of a 'pack of Camels' and 'Hershey bar' as currency (Amis 2014: 100). The allusions to America, made at the end of 2014 (the novel was published in September of that year), inevitably bring GTMO to mind. In March 2013, 39 of the 166 inmates went on hunger strike and the number had risen to 106 by July, with 45 being force fed. By December, when the Joint Task Force Guantanamo announced that it would cease disclosing information about the protests, 15 (all of whom were being force fed) were still on hunger strike (Associated Press 2013). President Obama renewed his efforts to close the concentration camp in 2014, but by the end of the year there were still 127 inmates (Jackson 2014). Amis' allusions to America, made in a context that is often nebulous, provides an extra dimension to the referential relation between representation and reality in fiction, suggesting a parallel between Auschwitz and GTMO that readers might otherwise not make. *The Zone of Interest* can be understood as a story about Auschwitz; as a story about Auschwitz in particular, but concentration camps in general; and as a story about Auschwitz in particular and concentration camps in general that makes indirect reference to GTMO. By means of these three literary devices, *The Zone of Interest* provides phenomenological knowledge of collaboration in genocide, representing what the experience is like and, in consequence, has criminological value in revealing motives of perpetration that would not be feasible for a nonfictional representation.

The Sheriff of Babylon

King and Gerad's (2018) *The Sheriff of Babylon* collects all twelve issues of the comic book series that was first published by Vertigo Comics in 2015. The first six issues were collected and published as *Bang. Bang. Bang.* (King and Gerads 2016) and the last six as *Pow. Pow. Pow.* (King and Gerads 2017). The graphic novel is set in Baghdad during the Coalition Forces (CF) occupation, beginning in February 2004 and concluding two months later. I take the Iraq War (2003–11) to be an unjust war on the grounds of widespread scepticism concerning its legality (see, for example: Ricks 2007; Chilcot 2016). Aside from the question of legality, there are also its consequences, which include the Iraqi Insurgency (2011–13), the Iraqi Civil War (2014–17), and possibly the Syrian Civil War (which began in 2011 and is ongoing at the time of writing). The Iraq War itself consisted of two phases, the invasion of Iraq by the CF (May 2003) and the insurgency against the CF's occupation (2003–11). I also take the CF occupation to be an uncontroversial instance of mass harm, on the basis that aside from its causal role in these events reliable estimates put civilian casualties during the invasion at approximately 3,750, but those during the insurgency at approximately 112,450 (Conetta 2003; Iraq Body Count 2019). Only one of the three protagonists of *The Sheriff of Babylon*, Christopher, collaborates in the mass harm of the occupation and my exploration of phenomenological value will focus on the representation of his lived experience.

King and Gerads employ literary and graphic devices to convey knowledge of what it is like to collaborate in the mass harm of the CF occupation of Baghdad and three of these are particularly relevant to the phenomenological value of the graphic novel. The first device combines the literary and the graphic, juxtaposing the three protagonists to structure the narrative and exploiting the mode of representation to distinguish the protagonists. Christopher is a former American police officer contracted to train Iraqi Police recruits for the Coalition Provisional Authority (CPA). His reason for being in Baghdad is his desire to atone for his failure to arrest one of the 9/11 suspects prior to the attack by training police officers to bring the chaos in occupied Iraq to an end. Christopher is defined by his actions. On the second page on which he appears, he is told that there is a young girl suspected of being a suicide bomber in one of the canteens in the Green Zone. While everyone else flees for safety, Christopher walks in, makes himself a sandwich, and starts talking to the girl. While he is sitting with her, a tactical unit bursts in and shoots her in the head.

There are two aspects to this incident that establish precedents for the narrative to follow. First, Christopher's attempt to do the right thing by talking the girl down is precisely what is responsible for her death: by placing himself in her vicinity, he caused the tactical team to kill her in order to prevent the loss of his life; had he not been in the canteen, they would have tried to negotiate with her. Second, readers never find out whether the girl did or did not have a bomb strapped to her torso. This lack of certainty and resolution is of course a representation of the circumstances in warfare, whether high or low in intensity. Christopher will continue to be the man of action, maintaining his calm and composure throughout, and his agency will bring the narrative to its troubling conclusion.

Sofia (an Anglicised version of Saffiya) is a young Sunni expatriate who has returned to Iraq to take what she considers her rightful place in a leadership role. Her grandfather was one of the founders of the Ba'ath Party but fell foul of Saddam Hussein, who murdered him and the rest of her family. She has spent her life in exile attempting to persuade the American government to invade Iraq and has some influence with both the CPA and the Iraqi Governing Council. She is a member of the Small Council for Iraqi Reconstruction and her aim is to become prime minister of post-invasion Iraq, a goal that requires careful handling of the Americans and the Shia and Kurdish Iraqi factions. Sofia is defined by colour, specifically the use of red. The first panel in which she appears shows her with a red handbag and red nails, followed by a red rose, red windows, the red blood of her miscarriage, and a duller red headscarf in her confrontation with Al-Qa'ida. This use of colour stands out from both of the main palettes employed by Gerads, the military greens and desert yellows. Nassir is a middle-aged Shia man who was formerly the highest-ranking Shia police officer in Baghdad. Unlike the Iraqi Army, the Iraqi Police was not disbanded by the CPA, but most police officers abandoned their posts once the CF arrived, in order to avoid being regarded as enemy combatants or being subject to reprisals by the civilian population (Perito 2011). In contrast to the other two protagonists, Nassir is not motivated by any greater goal (such as keeping the peace or leading the country), but simply the survival of himself and his wife, Fatima. He is a highly intelligent man, defined by his words, which he uses with economy, precision, and understanding. On the first page on which he appears, he describes both his character and the milieu in which the narrative takes place in a single sentence: "I am police, a man of the law, but there is no law" (King and Gerads 2018: 23). When Christopher first meets Nassir, he unwittingly repeats Nassir's words by asking, "I'm looking for police. Are you police?" (King and Gerads 2018: 37).

The second device is graphic, the immersive visual representation of the hyper-violent environment in which Christopher finds himself. The ways in which Gerads achieves this in the graphic novel are too numerous to discuss here so I shall restrict myself to two: the use of colour and the representation of sound. As previously discussed, Gerads uses two main palette colours, which blend into one another at times. The yellow, beige, and khaki recreate the atmosphere of the desert landscape of Iraq and the first double page spread of the graphic novel (pages 10–11) sets the visual tone of much of what follows. The second palette is a combination of green, olive, and chartreuse that recreates the atmosphere of the military and is first used in part two of the graphic novel (most notably in the double page spread on pages 34–35). In *The Sheriff of Babylon* the Green Zone really is green, not just in terms of safety but in terms of colouring that provides a continual reminder of the military occupation. Similarly, the Red Zone really is red, a place where blood is spilled and splashed all over the panels of the pages without warning, as deadly violence erupts and then immediately stops. This precarity is compellingly represented in the mortar attack that takes place in part nine (pages 185–87), where black panels with a single 'Pow' are interspersed with blurred pictures of Christopher and Sofia diving for cover in the dust. As noted previously, the comic series was originally collected in two parts, *Bang. Bang. Bang.* (King and Gerads 2016) and *Pow. Pow. Pow.* (King and Gerads 2017). There is no explicit division of the graphic novel into two halves subtitled by the two sets of repeated onomatopoeias, but they nonetheless play an important role in representing the hyper-violent setting of the story. In the first six parts of the novel, 'bang' is the only way in which the sound of a gunshot is represented. The word is of course used for its value as an onomatopoeia, in imitating the actual sound of a gunshot. In the second half of the graphic novel, all 'bang's are replaced by 'pow's, a more juvenile and innocent-sounding imitation of the *pop* of a gunshot. The change from *Bang. Bang. Bang.* to *Pow. Pow. Pow.* provides a contrast as the violence, which was already significant in the first half, escalates in the second half. Significantly, the first 'Pow' is not a gunshot, but the sound of Nassir smashing his interrogator's face into a tabletop (King and Gerads 2018: 154). Despite the apparently innocuous onomatopoeia the violence in this half of the graphic novel is more personal, more hands-on.

The third device that King and Gerads use to convey knowledge of what it is like to collaborate in the mass harm of the CF occupation of

Baghdad is literary, the use of a murder mystery plot. The intersecting and diverging interests of the three protagonists, set against the background of a Baghdad descending into an inferno of death and destruction, are loosely structured around a murder mystery – the murder of Ali Al Fahar, one of Christopher's police recruits. When Fahar's body is discovered, Christopher is unsure what to do and asks the sergeant from the morgue, "Does this place have a sheriff?" (King and Gerads 2018: 28). The answer is, of course, no and it is this vacant position that Christopher will fill in his quest to discover Fahar's killer. Christopher calls Sofia for help (they are lovers) and she puts him in touch with Nassir. Christopher and Nassir find that Fahar's family have been executed in their home. Nassir is then abducted by Abu Rahim, a foreign Al-Qa'ida commander who admits to killing Fahar and his family because they were traitors, working for the Americans, apparently bringing the case to an abrupt end with Rahim beyond Christopher's reach. Meanwhile, however, Sofia makes a deal with Franklin, who may be working for the CIA or the Defense Intelligence Agency (DIA), in which she will use herself as bait to trap Rahim. While Sofia and Nassir are awaiting Rahim's arrival, Christopher discovers that Fahar was a Naval Criminal Investigative Service (NCIS) agent whose mission was to infiltrate Al-Qa'ida and provide the NCIS with an opportunity to arrest or kill Rahim. The NCIS believed that Fahar had been turned by Rahim and let Rahim know that he was working for them, that is the NCIS set Fahar up for execution by Rahim in the hope that his murder would provide clues to Rahim's whereabouts. A Special Forces team bursts into Sofia's house, kills Rahim, and – it seems, once again – brings the central narrative to a close at the end of part eleven.

Part twelve begins several weeks later, with Christopher bumping into Jim, the CIA/DIA head of operations. Christopher abducts him at gunpoint and takes him to a remote location, where he is joined by Nassir and Sofia. Christopher's motivation remains undisclosed and Jim claims that he is merely a civilian IT contractor who is occasionally asked to pose as a senior intelligence officer because of his age. Nassir replies, "I believe you. It is not your fault", but then takes Christopher's pistol, continues, "But you are the one who is here", and executes Jim (King and Gerads 2018: 289). There is a suggestion that Christopher is trying to force the closure of the case regardless of whether that closure is appropriate. In other words, that Christopher is desperate to create some meaning from the series of violent events that have occurred by holding someone – anyone – responsible. The desire for closure within the narrative mirrors the reader's desire for closure in the experience of the narrative, but the murder mystery concludes without resolution. While it is clear that Rahim killed Fahar, it is unclear which organisation was responsible for setting up the murder. Similarly, it is unclear whether Jim really is a senior intelligence agent or whether Rahim really is an Al-Qa'ida commander. In fact, the truth behind almost all of the actions in the narrative remains unexplained. When one sets the confusion within the CPA in the context of the different motivations of the Iraqi factions the resulting chaos in Baghdad is revealed as inevitable. The combination of the three literary and graphic devices constitutes the phenomenological value of *The Sheriff of Babylon*, which is in virtue of the knowledge the graphic novel provides of what it is like to collaborate in the mass harm of a military occupation. This knowledge is provided by means of the representation of Christopher, whose participation in the occupation is motivated by a genuine desire to atone for his past failure. King and Gerads depict occupied Baghdad as not only a city without a sheriff, but an epistemic and moral vacuum where the only closure possible is arbitrary.

Conclusion

I began this chapter by identifying my argument for a criminology of narrative fiction as moving beyond the previous criminological engagements with fiction to demonstrate its aetiological role, fiction as a source of data about the causes of crime and social harm. The aetiological claim about narrative fiction is based on the phenomenological, counterfactual, and mimetic values of those narrative fictions, which often occur in combination, but which I deal with in isolation in order to make a convincing case for each. The subject of this chapter was thus the phenomenological element of the criminological value of narrative fiction. The phenomenological value of narrative fiction is the extent to which narrative fiction provides phenomenological knowledge of the causes of crime and social harm. Phenomenological knowledge is knowledge of what a particular lived experience is like. My interest is in phenomenological knowledge of the perpetrator of crime or social harm, that is knowledge of the lived experience of perpetrating crime or social harm, collaborating in crime or social harm, or facilitating crime or social harm. My claim is that some narrative fictions are sources of data of the perpetration, collaboration in, and facilitation of crime and social harm and that these narrative fictions can be employed in the same manner as any other source – as advancing the criminological project by explaining the causes of crime and social harm and, in consequence, having the potential to inform public policy and evidence-based practice.

In order to demonstrate this criminological value, I used two case studies, Amis' (2014) novel, *The Zone of Interest*, and King and Gerads' (2018) graphic novel, *The Sheriff of Baghdad*. Amis employs three literary devices to provide phenomenological knowledge of collaboration in the Nazi genocide of Jews, Jehovah's Witnesses, Roma, Eastern Europeans, the disabled, homosexuals, and socialists in 1939–45. The first of these is the combination of narrators (the three protagonists) with narration (in the first person), which provides direct access to the thoughts of the three perpetrators. Second, the three narrators are compared and contrasted in terms of their motivation for participating in the genocide, providing a range of selfish causes of collaboration. Third, Amis exploits the referential relation between representation and reality to suggest parallels between the concentration, extermination, and labour camps of Auschwitz and the detention camp in Guantanamo Bay. King and Gerads employ various literary and graphic devices in *The Sheriff of Babylon* to provide phenomenological knowledge of collaboration in the mass harm of the CF occupation of Iraq. I also focused on three of these, beginning with the juxtapositioning of the three protagonists – an American contractor, a Sunni expatriate, and a Shia police chief – whose interests diverge and intersect on multiple occasions as the narrative progresses. Second, King and Gerads provide an immersive representation of the sights and sounds of the hyper-violent environment in which the American protagonist, with whom I was primarily concerned, finds himself. Finally, the central plot of the narrative is a murder mystery, a genre that brings certain expectations from readers, which are subverted by King and Gerads in order to reveal occupied Baghdad as an epistemic and moral vacuum in which the consequences of actions cannot be predicted and in which meaning is arbitrary.

In each of the case studies, the combination of literary and/or graphic devices provides knowledge of the lived experience of perpetrating, collaborating in, or facilitating social harm. This phenomenological knowledge constitutes the phenomenological value of *The Zone of Interest* and *The Sheriff of Babylon* respectively and this phenomenological value is part and parcel of the works' respective criminological values in virtue of its aetiological character in each example. In both of these cases, the works provide phenomenological knowledge that is not available to nonfictional representations for reasons of access, ethics, or law. The phenomenological value of narrative fiction is not, of course, restricted to the particular knowledge I have articulated or to the two case studies I have employed, but can be found in many other exemplary narrative representations. Sticking to the examples I have used in this book so far, *Cop Land*, *Stander*, *The Godfather*, and *Queen of the South (season 1)* are all obvious candidates for providing knowledge of the lived experience of perpetrating, collaborating in, or facilitating crime. With my argument for the phenomenological value of narrative fiction concluded, I turn to counterfactual value in the next chapter.

5

Counterfactual Criminology

Introduction

Roman Polanski's *The Ghost* (2010) is a faithful adaptation of Robert Harris' (2007) novel of the same title. Harris' novel follows the formula established in two of his previous works, in which he combines the novelty of an alternative history with the suspense of a secret concealed at the core of that history. *Fatherland* (Harris 1992) is set in 1964, in a fictional reality where the Axis powers won the Second World War and Hitler, Heydrich, and Goebbels have managed to keep the majority of the population of the Greater German Reich ignorant of the multiple genocides the regime has perpetrated. In the final chapter, police detective Xavier March, who is being pursued by the Gestapo, discovers the ruins of Auschwitz concentration camp and realises that the conspiracy theories are true. The alternative history in *Archangel* (Harris 1998) is that Joseph Stalin had a son, who was brought up in the remote northern wilderness and whose psychopathic character traits were aggravated and honed for four decades. The secret stumbled upon by unscrupulous academic Fluke Kelso is that a reactionary Russian political faction is intending to place the son in the Kremlin, ushering in a new Stalinist regime at the end of the twentieth century. Polanski's *The Ghost* begins with the protagonist (an anonymous ghost writer, played by Ewan McGregor) being interviewed for the job of completing former UK Prime Minister Adam Lang's (played by Pierce Brosnan) memoirs, following the death of Mike McAra, his friend and aide. McAra was not a professional author and the ghost is required to rewrite the manuscript, in the course of which he investigates both the circumstances of Lang's life and the circumstances of McAra's death.

The ghost begins to suspect that Lang was recruited by the CIA while a student at the University of Cambridge. When he confronts Lang with the evidence he has uncovered, Lang denies the accusation emphatically. Shortly after, Lang is murdered by a former Army officer whose son was killed in Iraq, the memoirs are published, and the narrative appears set to conclude without a clear resolution, Lang a likely but unconfirmed CIA agent. In the last seven minutes (of 126) of the film, the ghost realises that the CIA agent is in fact

Lang's wife, Ruth (played by Olivia Williams), who was recruited while studying at Harvard University. He foolishly tells Ruth that he has discovered her secret and the narrative concludes with his assassination, minutes after the confrontation. Lang, McAra, and Ruth are thinly-fictionalised versions of Tony Blair, Alastair Campbell, and Cherie Blair respectively and Harris structures his story around an ingenious combination of Blair's subordinate relationship with the Bush administration and Cherie's lack of popularity with the British public. The alternative history is thus one in which Blair was working for the US government without his knowledge, being manipulated by his wife, who was his CIA handler. Polanski provides his audience with knowledge of a possible but non-existent situation that casts doubt on the historical reality in virtue of its explanatory power. Whether one takes the revelation that Ruth/Cherie is the agent as a final fictional twist or an actual historical implication, the suggestion that one or both of the Blairs was a CIA agent is not nearly as far-fetched as it may initially seem, as Christopher Bray (2007) acknowledges in his otherwise uncomplimentary review of Harris' novel: 'Even the book's shock-horror revelation – so shocking it simply *can't* be true, though if it were it would certainly explain pretty much everything about the recent history of Great Britain – comes about only because our man accidentally switches a sat-nav on.'

In the previous chapter, I used two case studies to demonstrate the phenomenological value of narrative fiction, Amis' (2014) *The Zone of Interest* and King and Gerads' (2018) *The Sheriff of Babylon*. The case studies were selected from different modes of representation, the literary mode of representation (Amis' novel) and a hybrid mode of representation (King and Gerads' graphic novel). Hybrid modes of representation combine two or more modes (such as literary and pictorial in the case of a graphic novel) and the cinematic mode of representation is essentially hybrid, as I noted in Chapter 2. Both of the case studies in Chapter 4 were concerned with state crime, which is more accurately described as social harm in virtue of the complexity of the legal issues involved (genocide, for example, was legal in Nazi Germany, but perpetrators were nonetheless prosecuted for crimes against humanity after the war). The two case studies I employ to demonstrate the counterfactual value of narrative fiction in this chapter are selected from the cinematic and the literary modes of representation. The first involves what Sandra Walklate (2017: 63) refers to as 'ordinary crime' – a term that is not intended to diminish the harm caused by this type of crime, but is indicative of the crimes that come to mind most readily when *crime* is used and the crimes that are standardly the subject of criminological inquiry – and the second state crime. The two case studies I employ to demonstrate the mimetic value of narrative fiction in the next chapter are both selected from the cinematic mode of representation and both involve crime (and social harm) committed by organised criminal enterprises. The point I want to make here is that there is no necessary relation among the criminological values (phenomenological, counterfactual, or mimetic) of narrative fictions, their various modes of representation (literary, cinematic, or hybrid), or the categories of crime or social harm (state, ordinary, or organised) about which they provide knowledge. Any mode of fictional representation can be valuable in any of the three ways about any of the three categories of crime. There is, however, a closer and stronger relationship between the cinematic mode of representation and mimetic value, which I discuss in Chapter 6.

This chapter proceeds with an explanation of counterfactual knowledge in terms of its relation to fictional realities, that is the sense in which counterfactual thinking and possible worlds are essentially fictional. I identify two distinct ways in which the representation of the possible but non-existent has criminological value: by providing knowledge of hypothetical situations that could not be reproduced in reality for legal or ethical reasons and by providing knowledge of alternative realities that casts doubt on knowledge of historical or contemporary reality. I then explore these counterfactual values by means of two case studies, which demonstrate the provision of the two kinds of counterfactual knowledge respectively. ITV's *Broadchurch (series 3)* (2017) provides knowledge of the social harm of rape myths and victim blaming by means of a detailed and complex exploration of the legal and moral responsibility for rape. Marlon James' (2014) novel, *A Brief History of Seven Killings*, provides knowledge of crimes committed in the name of the Cold War by representing an alternative history of Jamaica in which the CIA funded, armed, and trained organised criminal enterprises as part of the war on communism. Both the television series and the novel reveal causes of social harm and crime that would not be feasible for nonfictional representations. My conclusion is that in providing counterfactual knowledge of the causes of fictional crimes and social harms, the case studies provide explanations of the causes of actual crimes and social harms, data that could be employed in the reduction or prevention of those crimes and social harms.

Counterfactual knowledge

'Counterfactual' is used in both philosophy and psychology, most often employed in the context of possible worlds in philosophy and counterfactual thinking in psychology. David Lewis (1973) produced the first comprehensive philosophical analysis of counterfactuals, which he conceived as propositions that express conditionals that are contrary to fact. A conditional is a statement that takes the form *If ..., Then ...* and an example of a conditional that is contrary to fact is: if HOLMES (Home Office Large Major Enquiry System) had been available in 1975, then West Yorkshire Police would have charged Peter Sutcliffe with murder before January 1981. The conditional is contrary to fact, because HOLMES was not available until 1985 and Sutcliffe was not charged until after he had killed thirteen women 1975–80 (Bilton 2006). Lawrence Byford's (1981) report identified the inability of the Ripper Incident Room to cope with the vast amount of intelligence generated by the investigation as one of the reasons for the delay in catching Sutcliffe. Although the Police National Computer was used to a limited extent from June 1978 to August 1979, most of the reports were stored manually and it seems highly likely that relevant information from the Cross Area Sightings would have been retrieved much more quickly had information technology such as HOLMES been available. Lewis (1986) understands counterfactuals in terms of *possible worlds*, such that there is a possible world in which (in contrast to our world) Sutcliffe was arrested and charged prior to January 1981 and did not murder thirteen victims. In psychology, Daniel Kahneman (Kahneman and Tversky 1982) discusses counterfactuals as assessments, judgements, and fantasies that take alternatives to reality as their subject. Drawing on Lewis (1973), Kahneman (Kahneman and Miller 1986) explores *counterfactual thinking* in terms of knowledge of categories, the interpretation of experience, and the role of affect. A *counterfactual* can be defined as a circumstance that has not happened, but might, could, or would happen if conditions differed from those actually existing.

There is an obvious sense in which counterfactual thinking is essentially fictional, extrapolating from reality to an alternative to reality by recourse to the imagination. Daniel Dorhn (2009) also draws on the work of Lewis, using an example of his to demonstrate the relationship between fiction and reality exemplified in the counterfactual. Lewis (1983: 278–79) poses the question of whether a beggar could be dignified and suggests that narrative fiction could provide an answer that is not accessible to the conceptual analysis standardly employed by philosophers:

I find it very hard to tell whether there could possibly be such a thing as a dignified beggar. If there could be, a story could prove it. The author of a story in which it is true that there is a dignified beggar would both discover and demonstrate that there does exist such a possibility. An actor or a painter might accomplish the same. Here the fiction serves the same purpose as an example in philosophy, though it will not work unless the story of the dignified beggar is more fully worked out than our usual examples.

In response, Dorhn (2009: 40) claims that:

Lewis's example shows how literature may expand everyday capacities of counterfactual thinking. We cannot be sure how far the characteristics of being a beggar and of being dignified are metaphysically compatible. By imaginatively elaborating concrete characteristics of such a beggar in a counterfactual paradigm scenario, an author may sharpen our counterfactual intuitions.

Neither Ruggiero (2003) nor Frauley (2010) use 'counterfactual', but the concept is implicit in Frauley's (2010: 3) characterisation of fictional realities as an analytic tool in terms of 'a disciplined imagination'. The disciplined imagination is one of the means by which knowledge is acquired from fiction in the critical realist framework, linking text (literary or cinematic) to reality by the combination of linguistic (literary) or linguistic and pictorial (cinematic) structure, the analytic language of criminology, the practices of reading (literature) or viewing (cinema), and the extent to which fiction is characterised by truth as well as invention. I think Frauley is most explicit about counterfactual value in his discussion of literary and cinematic texts as empirical referents for criminological theories. Theory must be grounded in order to retain its criminological or sociological relevance, with Frauley (2010: 17) maintaining that 'theorizing ought to be guided by but not constrained by the empirical'. This guidance without constraint can be found in the fictional (or alternative) realities of literary and cinematic texts and the exemplification of theories and concepts is, in turn, achieved by the deployment of the disciplined imagination to these fictional realities. Recall from Chapter 3 that literary or cinematic texts are empirical referents for a theory when theories are exemplified in textured detail and the theoretical interpretation of the novel or film enhances the literary or cinematic experience. The example of

Frauley's I quoted is amenable to restatement in counterfactual terms in a variety of ways, one of which is: if Katz's (1988) moral transcendence is valid, then the process of symbolic transformation would occur as represented in *Falling Down*.

The *counterfactual value* of a representation is the extent to which that representation provides knowledge of reality by means of exploring alternatives to that reality. Counterfactuals can be distinguished in terms of their temporality, providing either retrospective or prospective knowledge of the significance of a variable. In the example of the Yorkshire Ripper, the comparison of the investigation with (imagined) and without (reality) HOLMES provides knowledge of the significance of HOLMES to cases that cut across police service boundaries. A prospective example would be a comparison of the extent to which the police services of England and Wales are representative of the communities they police with (reality) and without (imagined) the bachelor's degree entry requirement introduced in November 2018 as a means of achieving this end by 2025 (National Police Chiefs' Council 2016; College of Policing 2019). Daniel Hirschman (2018) sketches an argument for the counterfactual value of science fiction in particular, setting out five interconnections between the genre and sociological inquiry, in the course of which he delineates three kinds of counterfactuals. Tested counterfactuals are circumstances, practices, or theories that were actually pursued by a culture, society, or nation in the past but were quickly rejected or abandoned. Available counterfactuals are circumstances, practices, or theories that were available to a culture, society, or nation and were considered but not pursued. Both of these categories are retrospective in my terminology. In contrast, extreme counterfactuals were neither tested nor available, but are circumstances, practices, or theories that are so different from those in existence that they require an extensive engagement with the imagination for their very conception. Science fiction is, again necessarily rather than contingently, a source of extreme rather than available or tested counterfactuals. In my terminology, extreme counterfactuals are prospective.

Interestingly, Hirschman employs Amazon Studios' *The Man in the High Castle* (2015–19), which I discussed in detail in *Narrative Justice* (McGregor 2018b), as an example of an extreme counterfactual. He (2018: 13) claims that the series 'imagines a present-day U.S. situated in a world in which the Nazis won World War II'. In fact the series, like Philip K. Dick's (1962) original novel, begins in 1962. Furthermore, given Hitler's well-documented megalomania and the war of aggression pursued by the Empire of Japan against the US, it seems unlikely that an Axis victory was beyond the conception of either Hitler or Hideki and makes for a better fit with Hirschman's available category. From a criminological perspective, the most significant distinction between counterfactuals is concerned with the way in which they provide knowledge. The different ways in which counterfactuals provide knowledge is, in turn, related to Frauley's (2010) and my own concern with the precise relationship between reality and representation in narrative fiction. *Counterfactual knowledge* is knowledge of reality that is provided by the exploration of alternatives to that reality. With this in mind, I make a distinction between two kinds of counterfactual that cuts across and is more consequential than either the difference between retrospective or prospective counterfactuals or among tested, available, or extreme counterfactuals.

In the first, the narrative fiction represents a fictional world in which a particular set of circumstances, practices, or theories hold and invites the audience to respond to those circumstances, practices, or theories in a particular way by means of the narrative framework. Recall from Chapter 4 that the framework of an exemplary narrative is the preferred set (or sets) of cognitive, evaluative, and emotional responses to the narrative and that the reader or member of the audience that accepts this authorial or directorial invitation adopts the standard mode of engagement to the representation. Taking a term from Hirschman, I shall call this kind of counterfactual an *ideal counterfactual*: the narrative fiction presents an ideal, understood as the pairing of a particular set of circumstances and a preferred response to those circumstances. The relationship between representation and reality is in virtue of the fact that the knowledge provided for the fictional world holds for any actual world (past, present, or future) in which the ideal occurs. In Chapter 1, I mentioned Derek Raymond's (1984) *He Died With His Eyes Open*. The protagonist, an anonymous detective sergeant in A14 Unexplained Crimes, and the case he investigates are fictional, but the knowledge provided about the difficulties of ensuring justice for the alienated and anguished would (also) apply to any detective working in a society where inequality is high and egalitarianism low. The conveyance of this knowledge is a function of the referential relation between fictional works and the actual world that I have explained in terms of universals. In terms of the counterfactual value of a narrative fiction, an ideal counterfactual provides knowledge of reality by the exploration of alternatives to that reality because the subject of that knowledge is both the ideal in the fiction and any person, place, or event that approximates that ideal in reality. I shall use the example of ITV's *Broadchurch (series 3)* (2017) to demonstrate the criminological value of ideal counterfactuals.

The other kind of counterfactual is also reliant on the combination of the author or director's narrative framework and the standard mode of engagement of the reader or audience. Adapting Lewis' (1986) terminology, I shall call this kind of knowledge a *probable counterfactual*: the narrative fiction simultaneously represents an alternative to reality and suggests that this alternative may be partially or totally true, that the fictional explanation of circumstances, practices, or theory may be the actual historical or contemporary explanation. The example with which I began this chapter, Polanski's *The Ghost* (2010), is a case in point. In consequence of the fictional characters of Lang, McAra, and Ruth being obviously and closely based on Blair, Campbell, and Cherie the referential relation between the fictional work and the actual world is not just the usual universals or types (people like Lang, McAra, and Ruth), but the particulars or individual tokens of that type (Blair, Campbell, and Cherie). Similarly, the events represented – the manipulation of Lang while Prime Minister by Ruth, who is working for the CIA – refer not just to types of situations where a head of state appears to submit himself to the will of another head of state in the absence of coercion, but specifically to Blair's apparently subservient attitude towards the Bush administration in the US. In terms of the counterfactual value of a narrative fiction, a probable counterfactual provides knowledge of reality by the exploration of alternatives to that reality because the fictional alternative is represented as providing a possible, probable, or actual explanation of the historical or contemporary reality. I shall use the example of James' (2014) *A Brief History of Seven Killings* to demonstrate the criminological value of probable counterfactuals.

Broadchurch 3

Broadchurch (2013–17) is a contemporary crime drama produced by ITV (Independent Television) and set in Broadchurch, a fictional coastal town in the English county of Dorset (in the West Country). In keeping with the genre, the series follows a pair of police detectives, Detective Inspector Alec Hardy (played by David Tennant) and Detective Sergeant Ellie Miller (played by Olivia Colman) (Turnbull 2014). Each season consists of eight episodes of approximately 45 minutes duration.[1] Season 1 (*Broadchurch* 2013) focuses on the investigation of the murder of an eleven-year-old child. Season 2 (*Broadchurch* 2015) focuses on the consequences of two police investigations – the court case of the murder trial from the previous season and the protection of a witness from one of Hardy's earlier cases. Season 3 (*Broadchurch* 2017) focuses on a new crime, the rape of Trish Winterman (played by Julie Hesmondhalgh), and the consequences of the not guilty verdict in season 2 (for the murder investigated in season 1). All three seasons explore the effects of violent crime on the close-knit community of Broadchurch.

Broadchurch 3 begins with Trish reporting that she has been raped while at a party held by her friend, Cath Atwood (played by Sarah Parish), and her friend's husband, Jim Atwood (played by Mark Bazeley). While Trish was smoking outside, she was knocked unconscious, tied and gagged, moved to a more remote location, and raped. Hardy and Miller pick up the case, determining that Trish did not see the rapist and that the crime was premeditated. As the investigation progresses, suspicion falls on: Trish's husband, Ian Winterman (played by Charlie Higson), from whom she is separated; a recently-released sex offender, Aaron Mayford (played by Jim Howick); Clive Lucas (played by Sebastian Armesto), a sexually aggressive minicab driver; and Atwood, who had consensual sex with Trish on the morning of the party. Halfway through the season (at the end of episode 4), Laura Benson (played by Kelly Gough) comes forward, claiming that she was raped in a similar manner but did not report the crime because she was drunk and knew she would be blamed by the press and the public. As the pace picks up in the second half of the season, a third victim, Nira (played by Ellora Torchia), tells an Independent Sexual Violence Advisor that she may also have been raped by the same man. Nira did not report the rape initially and refuses to report it now because she does not want her family to know. Suspicion is focused on three men in turn: first Trish's employer, Ed Burnett (played by Lenny Henry), who is obsessed with her; then Atwood again (whose own wife suspects him); and finally on Leo Humphries (played by Chris Mason), a shopkeeper who is tangentially linked to several aspects of the extended investigation. In the final episode, Humphries is found to have raped three women previously (including Laura and Nira) and to have assaulted and bound Trish, but then coerced Lucas' teenage son, Michael (played by Deon Lee-Williams), to rape her. Humphries has been grooming Michael as a sexual predator and Lucas knows that his son and Humphries are responsible for the rape. From the point of view of the overarching plot of the series (which finishes with season 3), the conclusion brings the narrative back to the point at which it began, the horrific consequences of the crimes for Miller, as both a police officer and a member of the local community. Miller's husband, Joe (played by

Matthew Gravelle) was the child murderer in season 1, and her eldest son, Tom (played by Adam Wilson), is close friends with Michael. Although Tennant receives top billing, it is Miller rather than Hardy who is the protagonist of the series as she experiences the many and varied unpleasant consequences of the crimes that ripple through the community across the three seasons.

The ideal counterfactual knowledge of *Broadchurch 3* is provided by means of the integration of narrative content with narrative form, the combination of changes in the circumstances of the rape with changes in the framework from which Trish is viewed. The content reveals both the ubiquity of rape myths, false beliefs about sexual assaults that condone sexual aggression, and the propensity of the public for victim blaming (Brownmiller 1975). Episode 1 begins with Trish apparently the victim of what Jennifer Temkin, Jacqueline Gray, and Jastine Barrett (2018: 210) refer to as the ' *"real rape" stereotype*'; that is, the rape was violent, by a stranger, resisted by the victim (who is physically injured), and reported immediately. Across the next six episodes, however, this stereotype is broken down step-by-step, in the course of which many of the myths associated with rape – such as the relationship between alcohol and consent and the relevance of sexual history evidence – are revealed as part of the tacit acceptance of rape that remains prevalent in the twenty-first century (Grubb and Turner 2012; Temkin, Gray and Barrett 2018). First, Hardy and Miller realise that two full days have passed between the crime and its reporting (episode 1). Trish then delays the investigation further when she is reluctant to provide a full statement. She is also discovered to have been sexually promiscuous during her separation (episode 2). Flashbacks are used to confirm that Trish was drinking heavily at the party and to show that she was drunk and flirting with several men (episode 4). The connections between rape myth acceptance and racism are explored when suspicion falls on Burnett (episode 6) and the question of intimate partner rape is explored when suspicion returns to Atwood, her lover (episode 7) (Suarez and Gadalla 2010).

The narrative framework initially invites sympathy for Trish, employing dramatic and cinematographic means to emphasise her courage in reporting the rape to the police, subjecting herself to invasive procedures, and recalling the details of the assault. As the circumstances of the case drift away from the real rape stereotype, the perspective from which Trish is presented also changes, becoming gradually less sympathetic. Despite her initial cooperation, Trish impedes a difficult investigation when she postpones a formal interview and then, in the interview, refuses to identify the man with whom she had consensual sex before the party (episode 2). Aside from making Hardy and Miller's job more difficult, Trish's refusal leads to Atwood being accused of rape twice, first on the basis of DNA evidence and then when he is found to have met Laura. Under pressure, Trish reveals that she had sex with Atwood, who is her best friend's husband, for no reason other than sexual gratification and that she has no intention of confessing this betrayal of trust (episode 4). When Cath subsequently makes the reasonable request that Trish cease contact with her and her husband, Trish responds with aggression (episode 6). Trish's personality is performed to perfection by Hesmondhalgh, constituting a complicated combination of merits and flaws; being unquestionably brave and resilient, but also not particularly likeable, lacking in charisma, and prone to selfishness. At the same time as the audience is invited to regard the offence of which Trish is a victim as less serious so she is represented as less amiable.

The integration of the narrative content with the narrative form creates a cinematic experience in which members of the audience are invited to accept one or more rape myths at the same time as they acknowledge a growing distance between themselves and the victim of the crime. The complex plot twist in the final episode has a threefold significance: at the narrative level, the identification of an unexpected perpetrator sustains suspense; at the thematic level, the realisation that Humphries is a psychopathic serial rapist raises the stakes of the crimes for the community in general and Miller in particular; at the level of audience engagement, the conspiracy between Humphries and Michael constitutes a reversal of fortune in which the invitation to minimise the significance of the rape is disclosed as completely unjust. In other words, after having attempted to persuade the audience to either accept myths, judge Trish as blameworthy, or both, the studio shows rape myths and victim blaming to be misleading, unethical, and dangerous. The compelling and unambiguous message conveyed is that none of the counterfactual options explored would have changed either the legal or moral responsibility for the rape, both of which are exclusively borne by the perpetrators. The integration of content with form in the cinematic narrative constitutes an in-depth exploration of a violent sexual crime that would be precluded by legal and ethical considerations in nonfiction, providing ideal counterfactual knowledge of legal and moral responsibility for rape by representing a fictional situation. This knowledge consists of data that expose the appeal of rape myths and victim blaming and is criminological to the extent that the explanation of mythology and blame could be used to improve the way in which the criminal justice system deals with violent sexual crimes.

A Brief History of Seven Killings

Marlon James' *A Brief History of Seven Killings* was published in 2014 and won the Man Booker prize the following year. It is a long novel (686 pages) that represents a sequence of events that takes place in Jamaica and America from 2 December 1976 to 22 March 1991 and involves 69 different characters (a list of whom is provided between the contents and the two epigraphs). The book is written in the first person and narrated by twelve different characters, one of whom uses three aliases in addition to her real name. James does not use quotation marks to identify direct speech, which contributes to both the immediacy of the narrative, facilitating a seamless transition from semi-structured interior monologue to stream of consciousness, and its complexity, as the identity of the speakers is not always evident in the dialogues. There is potential for further confusion in that the first narrator, Arthur Jennings, is a ghost, murdered before the story starts. Jennings narrates the prelude and the last chapter of each part with the exception of the last. Excluding the prelude, there are 83 chapters divided into five parts, each of which is set during a single day: 'Original Rockers' (2 December 1976) is concerned with the preliminaries to the planned murder of Bob Marley by a group of eight men led by the gangster Josey Wales; 'Ambush in the Night' (3 December 1976) narrates the botched assassination and its immediate aftermath, including the death of two of the assassins, Demus and Bam-Bam; 'Shadow Dancin'' (15 February 1979) focuses on the repercussions of the assassination attempt in Jamaica, including the killing of three more of the assassins: Funky Chicken, Leggo Beast, and the only unnamed man; 'White Lines/Kids in America' (14 August 1985) is concerned with the consequences of the assassination attempt in America, particularly in New York, ending with Wales embarking on a shooting spree in a crack house and the murder of the sixth assassin, Weeper; and 'Sound Boy Killing' (22 March 1991), which concludes the narrative from the multiple perspectives of Luis Hernán Rodrigo de las Casas (a CIA contractor known as Doctor Love), Millicent Segree (actually Nina Burgess, a witness to the attempt on Marley's life), and Alex Pierce (a journalist who has been researching a book on the assassination attempt).

The probable counterfactual knowledge of *A Brief History of Seven Killings* is provided by means of two literary devices, each of which is complex, but whose complexity is exacerbated by their conjunction, imbrication, and convolution. The first device is the concealment of the referent of the title, of which seven of the multiple murders represented form the skeleton of the plot. The second device is the deliberate blending of fact and fiction and the combination of the devices makes it difficult to discern the thematic unity underlying what is at times a bewildering sequence of represented events. The storyline involving Pierce in the final part of the novel draws attention to the question of the referent of the novel's title. In the previous part, Pierce appeared to be researching a book on Jamaica, but when his narration resumes, he has just submitted part four of a seven part article on the crack house murders for *The New Yorker*, entitled 'A Brief History of Seven Killings'. He returns to his home in Washington Heights to find Eubie, the second-in-command of Wales' Storm Posse, and six gang members waiting for him (seven is a recurring number in the novel, making the referent of the title all the more opaque). Eubie has read the first three parts of the article and is concerned about mention of the Storm Posse, which originated in Copenhagen City (a fictionalised Tivoli Gardens, Kingston), operating in New York. He asks Pierce why he has called the article 'A Brief History of Seven Killings' when there were eleven and Pierce replies, 'Couldn't find any info on the other four. Besides, seven is a good round number' (James 2014: 656). Pierce's flippancy in the face of death may be motivated by a desire to conceal the real reason, but this is neither confirmed nor denied in the remaining chapter narrated by him. In Pierce's final chapter (82 of 83), he lets Eubie know that Wales fired the bullet that nearly killed Marley during the assassination attempt and Eubie reflects that seven of the eight assassins are now dead. This disclosure is succeeded by the following dialogue between Eubie (first speaker) and Pierce (second speaker):

— Pity. You want a story, there a story. Every single man but one who go after the Singer [Marley] end up dead.
— But Josey Wales not –
— The only one who might be alive, disappear in 1981 and nobody seem to know where he gone. But me.
— And where is that?
— You no seem too interested.
— No, I am. Really. Where is he?
— As I said, you not interested.
— And I'm saying I am. How do you know I'm not interested?
— Because I just tell you where him is. But don't fret yourself. This probably too big for you. One day somebody need to write a book about it.

— Oh. Okay.

— You go back to writing your *Brief History of Seven Killings*. (James 2014: 678)

The story to which Eubie initially refers, and the book he believes should be written, is the book that James has written, beginning with Wales revealing his links to the Jamaica Labour Party (JLP), the CIA, and the Medellín Cartel (chapter 6) – all independently of Papa-Lo, who is at the time the don of Copenhagen City – and ends with Wales' murder being confirmed on television news (chapter 83). The seven killings of the title of James' novel are the murders of seven of the assassins: Demus, Bam-Bam, Funky Chicken, Leggo Beast, the unnamed man, Weeper, and Wales. The title of the final part of the novel, 'Sound Boy Killing', refers to Wales' death and his personality is the force that drives the narrative, the impetus behind the assassination attempt, the takeover of Copenhagen City from Papa-Lo, and the expansion of the gang's operation to first Miami and then New York. When Wales' killing spree in New York brings unwanted attention from American law enforcement, he makes himself vulnerable to Eubie's ambitions and Eubie claims responsibility for Wales' subsequent murder in Kingston. These seven murders – amongst the many, many others that are either represented or mentioned in the narrative – provide the structure that James employs to tell the story of the rise and fall of Wales.

While this story is the subject of the novel at one level, that story is in turn underpinned by another, the CIA's involvement in Jamaican politics. Wales and others are trained as paramilitaries by the CIA and provided with military grade weapons as well as more direct assistance from 'advisers' such as Doctor Love (who is an explosives expert) in a similar manner to that in which the CIA had recruited a force to fight communist influence and target Che Guevara in the Congo in the previous decade (Weiner 2007). When the novel opens, Jamaica is led by the People's National Party (PNP), with Michael Manley as Prime Minister. The PNP has strong socialist leanings and is supported by Shotta Sheriff and the Eight Lanes (a fictionalised Matthews Lane, Kingston) gangsters. The next general election – which will be contested by the JLP, a nationalist party supported by Papa-Lo and Copenhagen City – is due in two weeks. The novel suggests that the CIA have been active in Jamaica since 1966 and represents the organisation as initiating the assassination attempt on Marley in order to prevent him from performing at the Smile Jamaica Concert, which has been organised by Manley to broker peace between the warring PNP/Eight Lanes and JLP/Copenhagen City factions in the lead up to the election. The US is seeking to oust the PNP in consequence of Manley pursuing closer links with Cuba and a more socialist agenda. Papa-Lo, who is arrested and detained before the assassination attempt in order to prevent his interference, belatedly recognises the CIA-instigated insurgency:

> Back to last December and January and every month till now [3 December 1976]. You look at certain things and they is just certain things. Look at them another way and certain things add up to one big thing, one terrible thing, all the more terrible because you never add them up before. (James 2014: 180)

Marley is monumentally popular in Jamaica, personally acquainted with both Papa-Lo and Shotta Sheriff, and highly influential in the political and social arenas despite being aligned with neither faction. As the election approaches, however, there is a perception that he is sympathetic to the PNP. Marley had also been critical of the US, capitalism, and colonialism in general and the CIA in particular in his music (Gane-McCalla 2016). Pierce reflects on the combination of the increased CIA presence in Kingston and the increase in tension between the two factions: 'Meanwhile, the Singer [Marley], never one to pull punches, sings Rasta don't work for no CIA. In Jamaica 2 + 2 = 5, but now it's adding up to 7. And all these loose strands knotting around the Singer like a noose' (James 2014:62). Wales has no interest in Cold War politics, but has a long-term plan to usurp control of Copenhagen City from Papa-Lo and to turn its organised crime into an international enterprise. He takes advantage of the weapons and training provided to increase his power, but his actual payment for the attempt on Marley's life is that the CIA will turn a blind eye to his trafficking of Medellín cocaine to Miami. As the years pass, Wales extends his network to New York and London and James represents him as being at least partly responsible for the crack cocaine epidemic in New York by 1985 (Farber 2019). Wales only becomes a subject of interest to American law enforcement after killing eleven people in his rampage in Brooklyn and even then, it takes almost six years before his extradition from Jamaica is authorised.

The suggestion that the CIA ignored narcotics importation to the US and withheld information from organisations such as the Drug Enforcement Agency is not only plausible, but likely given the accusations of direct CIA involvement in the same. The first of these was by journalist Gary Webb, in 1996, reporting on links between the CIA, the Contras (anti-communists in Nicaragua), and the crack cocaine epidemic in South Los Angeles in the nineteen eighties (Webb 1998). Webb (1998) subsequently published his investigation as a book, *Dark Alliance: The CIA, the Contras, and the Crack Cocaine Epidemic.* Details were denied and confirmed by the different parties involved, but the claims and counter-claims were conveniently brought to an end with Webb's suicide in 2004 (Grim, Sledge and Ferner 2014). James Ellroy (2001), who employs a similar combination of history and invention in *The Cold Six Thousand*, suggests that the CIA trafficked heroin from Vietnam to the black suburbs of Las Vegas in the mid-nineteen sixties (McGregor 2019). What James thus succeeds in doing is setting organised crime in Jamaica and beyond in the context of the Cold War and providing an alternative history in which the CIA was responsible for both the assassination attempt on Marley's life and the international rise to power of Jamaican drug trafficking gangs.

James deliberately blends fact and fiction in his characters, setting, and action. All of James' narrators are fictional (or fictionalised versions of real people) as are all of his characters, with the exception of Marley. Similarly, the names of some but not all places have been changed (such as Tivoli Gardens and Matthews Lane). The names of most of the organisations involved have not been changed and the geopolitical context of Jamaica and New York 1976–91 is actual rather than fictional. The pivotal event around which the narrative revolves – the attempted assassination – is similarly real, as are other events (Lazar 2014). The blend of fact and fiction not only provides an alternative history to the standard history, but an alternative history for which there is at least some evidence. As such, *A Brief History of Seven Killings* provides probable counterfactual knowledge, representing an alternative history in which the CIA is responsible for the rise of organised crime in Jamaica in the last quarter of the twentieth century and then suggesting that this alternative provides at least a partial explanation of the historical reality. The knowledge of violence in Kingston and drug trafficking in America provided by the novel directs attention to remote and invisible but nonetheless powerful causes of crime and social harm – in this case, the international power and influence wielded by the US, the residual colonialism facilitated by the Cold War, and the direct action sponsored by the CIA. Part of the significance of this probable counterfactual knowledge is that the crime and social harm caused by the CIA intervention might otherwise be accounted for by social or psychological causes.

James' combination of referential concealment and the blending of fact and fiction goes even further, however, directing criminological inquiry towards the criminal and socially harmful consequences of international conflict, particularly an extended and global international conflict such as the Cold War. In other words, whether or not James actually believes that the CIA were complicit in the crack cocaine epidemic, the way in which he represents this involvement is sufficiently convincing to direct criminological inquiry towards similar cases where social or psychological explanations may obscure the criminal and socially harmful consequences of foreign intervention in developing countries. One way of describing this is that in setting organised crime in Jamaica in the context of the Cold War, James situates criminal problems in the context of international politics. In consequence, the knowledge provided by the novel concerns both the causes of crime and social harm in Jamaica and New York in the last quarter of the twentieth century in particular as well as the role of international politics in crime and social harm causation in general. This knowledge consists of data that explain one of the relationships between international politics and organised criminal enterprises and is criminological to the extent that it could be used to reduce the crime and social harm caused by foreign intervention.

Conclusion

I began this chapter by setting out three aspects of each of the case studies I employ in support of my argument for a criminology of narrative fiction: criminological value (phenomenological, counterfactual, or mimetic), mode of representation (literary, cinematic, or hybrid), and category of crime (state, ordinary, or organised). I noted first that there is no unique or exclusive relationship among any of the values, modes, or categories and second that there is a closer relationship between the cinematic mode of representation and mimetic value (which I discuss in the next chapter). As such, my selection of case studies has primarily been guided by the case studies themselves, by the combination of criminological insight and the ingenuity with which that insight is conveyed. The focus of the chapter was on the counterfactual element of the criminological value of narrative fiction. The counterfactual value of narrative fiction is the extent to which narrative fiction provides knowledge of reality by means of exploring alternatives to that reality. Counterfactual knowledge is, in consequence, knowledge of reality provided by the exploration of alternatives to that reality. I distinguished between two kinds of counterfactual in narrative fiction, ideal and probable. Ideal counterfactuals pair a particular non–existent set of circumstances with a preferred response to those circumstances and provide knowledge of circumstances that approximate the ideal in reality. Probable counterfactuals simultaneously represent an alternative to reality and suggest that this alternative is partially or totally true, providing not just knowledge of types of people, places, or events but actual historical or contemporary people, places, and events.

In order to demonstrate the counterfactual element of criminological value, I used two case studies, the third season of ITV's *Broadchurch* (2017) and James' (2014) novel, *A Brief History of Seven Killings*. *Broadchurch 3* is an example of an ideal counterfactual and provides knowledge of the legal and moral responsibility for rape by means of the integration of narrative content with narrative form, specifically the combination of changes in the circumstances of the rape with changes in the framework from which the victim is viewed as the season progresses. The studio creates a cinematic experience in which the audience is encouraged to accept one or more rape myths before revealing those myths and the victim blaming with which they are associated as unambiguously irresponsible and unethical. *A Brief History of Seven Killings* is an example of a probable counterfactual, providing knowledge of both the causes of crime and social harm in Jamaica and New York in the last quarter of the twentieth century in particular as well as the role of international politics in crime and social harm causation in general. The distinction between representation and reality is blurred at the level of the novel's subject (which is about the rise and fall of the fictional gangster Josey Wales and about the likelihood of actual CIA involvement in Jamaican politics during the Cold War) and at the level of the characters, settings, and action (some of which are real, some of which are fictionalised versions of reality, and some of which are fictional).

In the case studies, cinematic and literary devices are employed to provide counterfactual knowledge of causes of crime and social harm by means of exploring alternatives to reality or, more accurately, by means of exploring the alternative reality of a narrative fiction. The counterfactual knowledge constitutes the counterfactual value of *Broadchurch 3* and *A Brief History of Seven Killings* respectively and this counterfactual value is part and parcel of the works' respective criminological values in virtue of its aetiological character in each example. In both of these cases, the works provide knowledge that is not available to nonfictional representation for reasons of access, ethics, and law. The counterfactual value of narrative fiction is not restricted to the particular knowledge I have articulated or to the two case studies I have employed, but can be found in many other exemplary narrative representations. Drawing on narrative fictions I have used in this book so far, *He Died with His Eyes Open* and *Falling Down* are examples of ideal counterfactuals and *The Ghost* and *The Cold Six Thousand* examples of probable counterfactuals. The former pair provide knowledge of circumstances that approximate murder investigations of the marginal and circumstances that exemplify Katz's moral transcendence respectively. The latter pair provide knowledge of Blair's subservient relationship with Bush and the CIA's involvement in drug trafficking during the Second Indochina War respectively. With my arguments for both the phenomenological and counterfactual values of narrative fiction concluded, I turn to mimetic value in the next chapter.

6

Mimetic Criminology

Introduction

The Coen brothers' *No Country for Old Men* (2007) is, like Polanski's *The Ghost* (2010), a faithful adaptation of the novel upon which it is based, published by Cormac McCarthy in 2005. The film begins with a voiceover by Sheriff Ed Tom Bell (played by Tommy Lee Jones) as the audience is shown a short scene in which one of his deputies arrests Anton Chigurh (played by Javier Bardem). The voiceover concludes as follows:

> The crime you see now, it's hard to even take its measure. It's not that I'm afraid of it. I always knew you had to be willing to die to even do this job. But, I don't want to push my chips forward and go out and meet something I don't understand. A man would have to put his soul at hazard. He'd have to say, okay ... I'll be part of this world. (*No Country for Old Men* 2007)

No Country for Old Men is set in Texas, near the border with Mexico, in the nineteen eighties, although the film reproduces the novel's timelessness to the extent that it is most accurately described as a Western. The plot is initiated when Llewelyn Moss (played by Josh Brolin) stumbles across the aftermath of a drug deal gone wrong while hunting, discovering five pickup trucks, eight dead men, one wounded man, and a cargo of heroin bricks. He tracks the tenth man, who left the scene on foot, and finds him dead with a briefcase full of ten thousand-dollar bundles of banknotes. Moss does what most people would want to do in the circumstances and takes the money. Later, when he is with his wife Carla Jean (played by Kelly Macdonald) in his trailer park home, he feels guilty for leaving the wounded man. He returns to the scene of the shootout that night, arriving simultaneously with more members of one of the cartels, which sets up the story as a pair of superimposed pursuits: Chigurh (who is a cartel hitman) of Moss for the purpose of recovering the money and Bell of Chigurh for the purpose of stopping the multiple murders he commits.

The Coens appear to exercise cinematic (or, perhaps more accurately, *fictional*) licence as they quickly establish a simple axis of goodness, evil, and neutrality. Moss is clearly an everyman, motivated primarily by self-interest, but a loving and loyal husband capable of extending his kindness to strangers. Chigurh is equally clearly the embodiment of evil, a psychopath who enjoys killing, placing himself at risk by both killing gratuitously and dragging out the death of his victims in order to savour their fear. As the narrative progresses, Bell emerges as a conscientious, shrewd, and brave law enforcement officer, perfectly attuned to life on the frontier, where he has been sheriff for three decades. Extremes of good and evil are of course very rare in real life and the film seems to stretch the imagination a little too far by bringing two together in a tale that otherwise represents the borderland between America and Mexico with exacting verisimilitude. The film is at its most realistic, however, where the audience least expects it, in its conclusion. After discovering Moss' body, Bell realises that he is not up to the challenge of arresting a man like Chigurh and that he cannot cope with the hyper-violence of the narcotics trade. He retires, Chigurh kills Carla Jean, and the last shot of Chigurh shows him walking away from the scene of a motor vehicle collision – to his freedom and to the next job for the cartel. In cinematic and other fictions, particularly those where good and evil are so simplistically represented, audiences expect to see good triumph, but in this story the embodiment of evil kills the everyman (and many others along the way) and escapes while the embodiment of goodness fails completely. In the representation this is surprising, perhaps even shocking, but of course in reality it is precisely what one would expect were a rural sheriff to pursue an experienced cartel hitman. The film ends with Bell retired, recounting a dream about his future death to his wife. The ending recalls W.B. Yeats' (1928) 'Sailing to Byzantium', a poem that describes the passage into old age and from which McCarthy took the title of the novel. In structuring the narrative in this way, the Coens provide the audience with detailed and accurate knowledge of the everyday reality of the heroin trade in Texas in the nineteen eighties in particular as well as changes to criminal culture in general.

In my introduction to the previous chapter I discussed the relationship between the three modes of representation (literary, cinematic, hybrid) of the case studies and the three categories of crime and social harm (ordinary, state, and organised) about which they provide knowledge. I stated that any of the three modes of fictional representation can be valuable in providing any of the three types of knowledge (phenomenological, counterfactual, mimetic) about any of the three categories of crime, but noted that there is a closer and stronger relationship between the cinematic mode of representation and mimetic knowledge than between the literary or hybrid modes of representation and mimetic knowledge. This robust relationship is in virtue of the characteristic realism of the cinematic mode of representation, which I explain later. In consequence of the characteristic realism of the cinematic mode of representation, the most convincing demonstrations of the way in which narrative fictions provide mimetic knowledge are to be found in feature films and television series and I make use of two examples of the former for the case studies in this chapter. This is not to say that literary and hybrid representations cannot provide mimetic knowledge (*The Sheriff of Babylon*, for example, provides detailed and accurate knowledge of the causes of social harm during the CF occupation of Iraq), but that both modes are restricted in ways that the cinematic mode is not. The robust relationship between mode of representation and type of knowledge provided is unique to mimetic knowledge as there is no equivalent with respect to either phenomenological knowledge or counterfactual knowledge. In other words, there is no reason that a cinematic representation should be any better in providing phenomenological or counterfactual knowledge than a literary or hybrid representation, but the characteristic realism of the cinematic mode of representation provides cinematic representations with an advantage over and above literary and hybrid representations with respect to the provision of mimetic knowledge.

This chapter proceeds with an introduction to mimesis in which I distinguish between two related denotations of the concept, re-creation and imitation. I explain mimesis as re-creation in terms of the characteristic realism of the cinematic mode of representation, which is in turn a function of the combination of seven distinct kinds of realism associated with cinematic representation. I explain mimesis as imitation next, showing how the cinematic mode of representation combines re-creation with imitation to provide detailed and accurate knowledge of everyday reality unmatched by other modes of representation. I then explore the mimetic value of narrative fiction by means of two case studies, each of which demonstrates the provision of mimetic knowledge by cinematic fictions. Michael Mann's *Miami Vice* (2006) provides knowledge of the power dynamics of organised criminal enterprises by means of the combination of cinematography, acting, and structure. Fernando Meirelles and Kátia Lund's *City of God* (2002) provides knowledge of the complexity of the relationship between organised criminal enterprises and the communities within which they operate by means of an intricate narrative architecture composed of four levels of self-reflexive storytelling. Both feature films reveal causes of crime and social harm that would not be feasible for nonfictional representations. My conclusion is that in providing mimetic knowledge of the causes of fictional crimes and social harms, the case studies provide explanations of the causes of actual crimes and social harms, providing data that could be employed in the reduction or prevention of those crimes and social harms.

Mimetic knowledge

Mimesis is the re-creation or imitation of reality and the two denotations reflect two types of interest in mimesis that are relevant to criminological inquiry, the aesthetic and the anthropological. The aesthetic interest in mimesis as the re-creation of reality has been central to the practice of the fine arts and the conventions of representation in Europe for over two millennia. Classical theories of artistic production and reception maintained that mimesis was not only the purpose of art, but afforded works of art their characteristic value (Plato 1997; Aristotle 2004). The link between the value of art and representation on the one hand and accuracy, correspondence, likeness, realism, verisimilitude, and vividness on the other hand was not challenged until first the Romantic Era's focus on the artistic expression of genius (Kant 1790; Coleridge 1817) early in the nineteenth century and then the modernist focus on the formal features of representation early in the twentieth century (Bell 1913; Shklovsky 1921). Doubts about the aesthetic value of mimesis were matched by the development of the anthropological interest in mimesis as imitation, as either a biological faculty or a social practice (Bleek 1869; Darwin 1871). In the twentieth century, the anthropological interest gained ground in first critical theory (Benjamin 1933a, 1933b; Horkheimer and Adorno 1947; Adorno 1966) and then sociology (Girard 1978; Irigaray 1985; Bourdieu 1980; Taussig 1993).

The focus of my interest in mimesis is the aesthetic, specifically the conventions employed to re-create reality, although I shall also discuss the way in the which the cinematic mode of representation integrates the anthropological with the aesthetic by exploiting at least one evolutionary process during the cinematic experience. The aesthetic interest in mimesis – mimesis as re-creation – is usually explained in terms of *realism*. As Kendall Walton (1990: 328) notes, however, realism 'is a monster with many heads desperately in need of disentangling'. The first disentanglement to make is to distinguish aesthetic realism, which is concerned with the conventions employed to re-create reality in representation, from scientific realism, which is an ontological and epistemological approach to research (as discussed in Chapter 2). Aesthetic realism as I shall refer to it here is neither concerned with whether an objective reality exists nor with the extent to which an objective reality, if it does exist, can be known by scientists. It is, instead, concerned with the conventions of representation employed to re-create reality (whether objective, subjective, or intersubjective) and standardly involves characterising representations by means of some combination of the following adjectives: accurate, corresponding, lifelike, natural, resemblant, true to life, verisimilar, vivid, serious, everyday, ordinary, concrete, historicising, and socially inclusive. Aesthetic realism has been explored from both theoretical and philosophical perspectives.

André Bazin (1958: 21) is probably the best-known film theorist identified with realism and associated realism in the arts – including cinematic art – straightforwardly with resemblance, championing what is now known as the deep focus style over the montage style on the basis of the former's 'integral realism': its ability to reproduce reality as it is rather than reality as it is interpreted by the director. Siegfried Kracauer (1960) is acknowledged as being responsible for the first systematic and ultimately the most comprehensive realist film theory. Like Bazin's, Kracauer's realism was based on the photographic medium of the cinematic art form. Kracauer's (1960: 255) *cinematic realism* was in fact *camera-realism* and his clearest definition of the concept is presented in his definition of *the true film artist*, who

> may be imagined as a man [*sic*] who sets out to tell a story but, in shooting it, is so overwhelmed by his innate desire to cover all of physical reality – and also by a feeling that he must cover it in order to tell the story, any story, in cinematic terms – that he ventures ever deeper into the jungle of material phenomena in which he risks becoming irretrievably lost if he does not, by virtue of great efforts, get back to the highways he has left.

Bazin and Kracauer were concerned exclusively with the photographic element of film, which has become considerably less significant following the widespread introduction of computer-generated imagery (CGI) at the beginning of the twenty-first century (McGregor 2013).

Both the phenomenological-hermeneutic and analytic traditions were relatively slow to turn their attention to film as the subject of philosophical reflection. Gilles Deleuze (1983, 1985) published a philosophy of film in two parts in the phenomenological-hermeneutic tradition and Gregory Currie (1995) published the first systematic cinematic aesthetics in the analytic tradition. Currie defines his philosophy of film as realist on the basis of his stance on three theses: illusionism, transparency, and likeness. There are two types of illusions associated with film, cognitive and perceptual, and Currie rejects both. He first dismisses the '*Imagined Observer Hypothesis*', the claim that the viewer believes that she occupies the position of the camera and is therefore present in the story (Currie 1995: 167). He then dismisses the perceptual illusionist thesis, which is that the movement of images onscreen is illusory. *Transparency* was a term used by Walton (1984) to describe what Currie (1995: 48) calls the 'Presentation Thesis', the idea that photographs present rather than represent their subjects which he also rejects. Currie (1995: 79) endorses likeness as central to cinematic ontology and argues that: 'Likeness is a coherent thesis, and that it is possible to achieve a considerable degree of this kind of realism in film.'

Berys Gaut (2010) sets out a taxonomy of seven distinct kinds of realism that are relevant to cinematic representation (whether documentary or fictional):

(1) Content realism: the characters, settings, and action in a fictional representation are of a kind that exists in reality.
(2) Photorealism: the animated image of a character, setting, or action in a representation is indiscriminable from a photographic image of the character, setting, or action.
(3) Ontological realism: a photographic image has a causal rather than intentional relation to that which is represented because the representation is created by the capture of light waves emanating from that which is represented.
(4) Epistemic realism: a photographic image offers strong although not conclusive evidence that that which is represented existed at the time the photographic representation was created.
(5) Perceptual realism: the characters, settings, and action in a representation look (and sound) like their counterparts in reality.
(6) Transparency: a photograph presents rather than represents its subject; that is, the viewer sees the subject itself rather than a representation of the subject.
(7) Anti-illusionism: cinematic representations do not standardly create an illusion in the minds of their spectators.

Gaut (2010) makes a convincing case that (1) to (5) are all characteristic of cinematic representation. He argues that (6) and (7) are not characteristic of cinematic representation, but both claims are controversial, with arguments to the contrary being made by Walton (1984) and myself (McGregor 2018a). My position is that (1) to (7) are all characteristic of the cinematic mode of representation, in consequence of which the cinematic mode of representation is characteristically realist. When one compares cinematic representation to other, similar, modes of representation – such as pictorial, photographic, and theatrical – in terms of (1) to (7), it is obvious that cinematic representation has the greatest scope for realism. Pictorial representations can be realistic in terms of (1), (2), (5), and (7), but only a small class of pictorial representations – such as courtroom and crime scene sketches – are realistic in terms of (4) and none in terms of (3) and (6). Theatrical representations may be realist in terms of (1), (5), (6), and (7) but as there is no imagery involved (2) to (4) are not applicable. Photographic representations can be realist in all seven senses, but cinematic representations have a much greater scope for (5) because they can represent both the movement and the sound of that which is represented. With respect to mimesis as re-creation, the cinematic mode of reproduction is so realistic that it appears to reproduce rather than represent reality.

Robert Sinnerbrink (2016) comments on the complication, confusion, and conflation involved in the various uses of 'empathy' and 'sympathy'. He (Sinnerbrink 2016: 92) recommends distinguishing the terms as follows: 'sympathy as *feeling for* someone while empathy is *feeling with* him or her.' In other words, I sympathise by experiencing sadness when I realise that Moss' act of kindness initiates the chain of events that will cause both his and Carla Jean's deaths in *No Country for Old Men*, but I empathise with Moss when I experience surprise and fear at his pursuit by the cartel (that is, the same emotions that he experiences, albeit to a much lesser extent). All three modes of narrative representation I have discussed thus far can employ frameworks that establish a standard mode of engagement involving either sympathy, empathy, or a combination of the two and a framework that elicits the emotions of the audience is an essential element of the process by which a sequence of events is formed into a(n exemplary) narrative. Sinnerbrink, who is also concerned with the cinematic mode of representation, suggests that the complexity of the relationship between sympathy and empathy can be overcome by considering them as opposite poles along a single continuum of affective response. He (Sinnerbrink 2016: 95) identifies '*cinempathy*' as the movement along the sliding scale between these poles that typically occurs during the course of the cinematic experience in consequence of the combination of cinematography and characteristic realism.

In contrast, Murray Smith (2017) is eager to provide a precise distinction between empathy and sympathy, because the former involves lower level, pre-reflective responses that have an evolutionary origin. Mirror neurons are a type of neuron that is activated while executing or observing a particular action and human beings possess an extensive system of these neurons (Iacoboni 2008). Smith maintains that the mirror system reveals the neural underpinning of motor and affective mimicry and that understanding the emotions of others in this way is an instantiation of direct experiential knowledge. The mimicry of emotions and actions provides a scaffold upon which the imagination can build, in consequence of which the mirror system facilitates the creation of elaborate and exact empathic responses. Motor and affective mimicry can occur through facial expression: 'When we witness legible instances of the facial expression associated with certain basic kinds of affective state – the so-called "basic" emotions ... – we are apt to simulate the feeling associated with the expression, via the mechanism of facial feedback' (Smith 2017: 179). This mechanism has been exploited by film and television directors in various ways, most obviously in the use of close-up shots of the facial expressions of actors. *No Country for Old Men*, for example, concludes with a four second close-up of Bell's face in which the basic emotion of sadness is clearly legible, but which in the context of the overarching narrative and the scene in which the shot appears is more accurately described as a combination of bewilderment, shame, and anxiety. For Smith (2017: 183), the emotional response of the audience in sympathy is asymmetrical as the characters 'are responding to one situation but we are responding to their response to that situation'. Moss is surprised and afraid when he is ambushed by the cartel and I respond sympathetically by feeling sad.[1] The facial feedback I receive in the final shot of the film is, however, likely to cause me to mimic Bell's bewilderment, shame, and anxiety and to employ my imagination to the extent that I feel his bewilderment, shame, and anxiety. Smith's claim is thus that directors combine the anthropological and aesthetic interests in mimesis, exploiting the capacity of film to re-create reality in order to manipulate the emotions of audiences by means of evolutionary imitation.

Whether one considers the utilisation of cinematic realism in terms of Sinnerbrink's stimulation of audience emotion (re-creation) or Smith's stimulation and simulation (re-creation and imitation), the close relation between mimetic value and the cinematic mode of representation to which I referred previously is explained. The *mimetic value* of a representation is the extent to which that representation provides knowledge of the world by representing everyday reality in detail and with accuracy. *Mimetic knowledge* is knowledge of everyday reality that is detailed and accurate. My view is that Smith makes a convincing case for the intersection of the anthropological and aesthetic interests in mimesis in the cinematic mode of representation. The provision of mimetic knowledge is by no means restricted to the cinematic mode of representation, but feature films and television series have a greater potential to provide mimetic knowledge in virtue of their combined capacity for re-creation and imitation. If one is not convinced by Smith, Sinnerbrink's combination of characteristic realism and cinempathy is sufficient to explain the close relation between mimetic value and the cinematic mode of representation, on the basis of re-creation alone.

Miami Vice

Miami Vice (2006) is a paradigmatic example of a work of fiction that provides knowledge of organised crime by means of the explicit and extensive reproduction of its everyday reality on screen. *Miami Vice* (1984–90) was an action adventure television series that was produced by NBC (National Broadcasting Company) and ran for 112 episodes across five seasons from September 1984 to January 1990 (Lyons 2010). The series was set in Miami and followed the exploits of the Miami-Dade Police Department's Narcotics Bureau, focusing on two protagonists: Detective Sergeants James 'Sonny' Crockett (played by Don Jonson), a Vietnam veteran, and Ricardo Tubbs (played by Philip Michael Thomas), a former New York police detective. Mann was executive producer of the series and his feature film reprised the main characters, Colin Farrell playing Crockett and Jamie Foxx playing Tubbs. The plot of the film is loosely based on the pilot episode of *Miami Vice (season 1)* (1984), with one significant change, the introduction of Isabella (family name never revealed, played by Gong Li) in a major role. Following from the series, the film is concerned with the undercover work of Lieutenant Martin Castillo's (played by Barry Shabaka Henley) detective squad and opens with a scene in which Crockett and Tubbs discover that an undercover operation run by the Federal Bureau of Investigation against the Aryan Brotherhood in Miami has been compromised. As Miami-Dade were not part of the interagency task force running the operation, Castillo is asked if his squad can take over the case in order to identify both the source of the narcotics being trafficked and the mole within the justice system.

The plan is that the squad will first disable the go-fast boat service being used to import the narcotics and then offer their own service as a replacement.

One of the themes that pervades the film is the power wielded by the top echelons of organised crime which, in the context of Miami, is focused on South American cocaine cartels. In the film, the theme encompasses both the absolute control and complete unaccountability of the senior management, foregrounding the difficulty of bringing anyone other than those involved at the selling or trafficking level to trial. This is an international problem in policing: transnational criminal organisations are able to prevent witnesses providing evidence in court and to maintain a safe distance between their leadership and the illegal transactions (Von Lampe 2015; Antonopoulos and Papanicolaou 2018). In consequence, much narcotics enforcement is symbolic of police commitment rather than effective in crime reduction and one of the narrative devices by which tension is maintained in *Miami Vice* is the desire of Crockett and Tubbs to remain undercover for as long as possible in order to secure prosecutions higher up the chain of cartel command (Coomber, Moyle and Mahoney 2019). The invulnerability of the upper echelons of organised crime is confirmed in the last few minutes of the film. While Crockett and Tubbs snatch victory from the jaws of defeat in a dramatic police operation in Miami, Special Forces raid the jungle headquarters of Jesus Montoya (played by Luis Tosar), the apparent head of the cartel, in what is probably Colombia (the location is never confirmed). In a very short scene (under 30 seconds), dozens of soldiers burst into Montoya's mansion to find that everyone and everything in it (except the furniture) has disappeared, with evidence that the exodus happened in a hurry. The scene I want to focus on, which begins in the thirty-eighth minute (of 124) and is just under five minutes in length, demonstrates the way in which the film provides knowledge of the absolute power wielded by organised crime by means of the detailed and accurate reproduction of everyday reality.

After having been put in touch with the cartel by a confidential informant of Detective Trudi Joplin (played by Naomie Harris), Crockett, Tubbs, and several other detectives fly to Haiti posing as a trafficking gang. They are first interviewed by José Yero (played by John Ortiz), the cartel's head of counter-intelligence, and then Isabella, the cartel's head of finance. At the end of the second interview, Isabella tells them that they must now "meet the man" (*Miami Vice* 2006). Crockett and Tubbs are separated from the rest of their team and taken by motorcade to an undisclosed location in Port-au-Prince at night. As they approach their destination, they notice that all mobile phone signals have been disrupted, suggesting considerable technological expertise on the part of the cartel. The motorcade passes (without stopping) through what seems to be a military roadblock and arrives in a deserted car park, where it is received by men in civilian clothes armed with automatic rifles. The detectives are searched thoroughly and relieved of their handguns. They are then told to walk towards three trucks in the middle of the car park, across a killing ground of a hundred metres or more, while covered by armed men at both ends and a sniper on a rooftop overhead. On arrival, they are directed to a luxury SUV and instructed to sit opposite Isabella and Montoya. The interview that takes place is a monologue by Montoya (with one contribution by Isabella) as he sets out the conditions of their probationary period with the cartel. Montoya is clear about both the terms of their employment and the benefits of working for him: "In this business with me, I do not buy a service I buy a result. If you say you will do a thing, you must do exactly that thing. Then you will prosper beyond your dreams and live in Miami in millionaire style." (*Miami Vice* 2006) He continues to speak and the camera focuses on the jewel-encrusted watches both he and Isabella are wearing, visual evidence of the verbal claim.

The interview finishes on an apparently innocuous note, delivered by Tosar with a sinister inflection, "I extend my best wishes to your families. Thank you for making this trip to see me" (*Miami Vice* 2006). In the circumstances depicted thus far – the complete powerlessness of Crockett and Tubbs – the disjunction Montoya is establishing is clear: either follow your orders to the letter and become millionaires or deviate from your orders and have your families killed. After thanking them, Montoya indicates the door with a curt inclination of his head and they are dismissed without having said a word. They have not been asked any questions because Montoya is not interested in them as human beings only as a means to the end of trafficking narcotics to Florida. The purpose of the interview is less to communicate the details of the trial run (part of which were revealed by Isabella in the previous interview) than to establish the real conditions of employment: in coming to the cartel, Crockett and Tubbs have yielded all autonomy to Montoya, and are now faced with either compliance and wealth or non-compliance and death. The scene ends with the detectives, still under armed guard, watching the three trucks leave. Crockett and Isabella exchange a lingering look, foreshadowing the romantic relationship that will develop between them. The whole scene as described lasts for only four minutes and 24 seconds, but is able to convey a vast amount of detail by means of the combination of visual and verbal representation typically employed in film, integrating features such as cinematography with the non-verbal communication made by the actors. The advantage of representing such a scene by cinematic rather than literary representation is that the audience can acquire a great amount of perceptual information in a very short amount of time. If, for example, an equivalent scene in a novel attempted to convey the same amount of explicit and implicit information, the lengthy descriptions required would be tedious and detract from its drama – which is itself employed to provide information about the power dynamics of organised crime.

The detailed and accurate information about the power dynamics of organised crime is not merely revealed in this scene considered in isolation, but in the place of the scene within the complete fictional narrative. Montoya's power as displayed 40 minutes into the narrative is juxtaposed with the enacting of that power 40 minutes from the end of the film. Yero has never trusted Crockett and Tubbs, is jealous of Isabella's seniority in the cartel, and decides to betray Crockett and Tubbs in order to usurp Isabella. Without realising that they are all undercover police officers, he has his Aryan Brotherhood allies kidnap Joplin (who is having a relationship with Tubbs) and renegotiate the terms of the delivery on which Crockett and Tubbs are working. In a short sequence that switches between the ship the detectives have appropriated and the trailer park where Joplin is being held, one of the Brothers phones Crockett, using a television news broadcast to let him know that Joplin is both alive and in their custody. This development heightens the suspense of the film as the goal of the police operation switches from arrest to rescue. The juxtaposition of these two events in the narrative – the interview and the telephone call – forms a pattern of meaning that provides more information about the exercise of absolute power than either event on its own. The placing of the scene and sequence in the structure of the film are indicative of the value of cinematic fiction in particular.

The cinematic mode of representation is characteristically realist, in consequence of which both fictions and documentaries have considerable mimetic potential. What fictional representations (cinematic and other) can achieve with much greater ease than documentary representations is the creation of layers of implicit meaning in addition to the explicit information conveyed. In my example, Mann has the freedom to place the interview at 40 minutes from the beginning of the film and the telephone call 40 minutes from the end of the film precisely because the events being represented are fictional: he is not restricted by an actual sequence of events that must be reproduced on screen. While the details that are usually associated with mimetic value are not unique to cinematic fictions, the mimetic value of cinematic fictions is realised in different ways to documentary representations; for example, fictions are less accurate in the sense of not representing actual events, but more accurate in communicating information by formal as well as substantive means. To this structural element of mimetic value, one should add the ability of cinematic fictions to overcome the access, legal, and ethical obstacles that documentaries might face. Even with the contemporary technology available in terms of miniature and satellite cameras, it would be impossible to reproduce a meeting between cartel leadership and new employees at the level of detail provided in Mann's fiction. *Miami Vice* employs stylistic and structural cinematic devices to provide mimetic knowledge of the power dynamics of organised criminal enterprises, that is detailed and accurate knowledge of the absolute power wielded by the senior management. This knowledge consists of data that explain the motives for working for organised criminal enterprises and has criminological value to the extent that it could be used to reduce the influence and capability of those enterprises.

City of God

Meirelles and Lund's *City of God* (2002, *Cidade de Deus* in the original Portuguese) is based on historical events, being a cinematic adaptation of Paulo Lins' (1997) novel, *City of God* (*Cidade de Deus*), which is in turn a fictionalised autobiography focusing on the author's childhood in Cidade de Deus, a suburb of Rio de Janeiro that is often erroneously referred to as a *favela*. Janice Perlman (2010) draws attention to the misuse of '*favela*' as a catch-all term for all informal or irregular settlements in Brazil. *Favelas* are unplanned informal settlements typically consisting exclusively of detached houses, a feature they share with the wealthiest *bairros* (legitimate neighbourhoods) of urban Brazil. *Loteamentos* are settlements that are planned in advance and subdivided into grid patterns, but which occupy the land illegally. *Conjuntos* are housing developments built by the government for former *favela* residents, but are not considered part of the formal city. As such, Cidade de Deus is a *conjunto*, constructed in the West Zone of Rio in the mid-nineteen sixties as part of an official programme of forced *favela* removal in the city centre (Dulles 1996; Perlman 2010). Lins arrived in Cidade de Deus in 1966, when he was seven, and spent 30 years there as first a resident and then a researcher for urban anthropologist Alba Zaluar (Schwarz 2001).

Criminological analyses of *City of God* have drawn attention to the mimetic value of the film in virtue of the following features: its authenticity in being based on Lins' autobiography, which is in turn a product of his status as both a resident in and researcher of Cidade de Deus; the realistic representation achieved in virtue of the majority of the actors being amateur *conjunto* and *favela* residents encouraged to improvise; and the use of Cidade Alta, a *conjunto* in Rio's North Zone, as the location for filming (Diken and Laustsen 2007; Rafter and Brown 2011; McClennen 2011). All of these features contribute to the sense in which the people, places, and events represented in *City of God* correspond with the everyday reality of life in Cidade de Deus (and perhaps other *conjuntos* in Brazil). My discussion of the mimetic value of the cinematic fiction will focus on its narrative form, specifically on the way in which the story of these *conjunto* residents is told. Despite what appears to be an overriding realism in directorial intent, Meirelles and Lund explicitly draw attention to the act of invention that takes place when historical sequences of events are represented as narratives – the phenomenon I discussed in Chapter 1 in my rejection of the existent/invented dichotomy as means of distinguishing nonfiction from fiction. The directors combine this self-reflexive storytelling with an intricate narrative architecture to provide mimetic knowledge of the motivations for collaboration in and cooperation with organised criminal enterprises, that is detailed and accurate knowledge of the obstacles to resistance to organised crime.

City of God is 119 minutes long from beginning to credits, the cinematic autobiography of Wilson Rodrigues (known as Rocket and played by Luis Otávio as a child and Alexandre Rodrigues as an adult), a fictionalised version of Lins who aspires to be a photographer (in contrast to Lins' realised ambition to become a writer). Rocket narrates his own story in a voiceover and only reveals his identity as Rodrigues in the final shot of the film before the end credit sequence, in which the caption 'BASED ON A REAL STORY' also appears (*City of God* 2002). The film begins in the mid-nineteen sixties and follows the maturation of Rocket and Li'l Zé (played by Douglas Silva as a child and Leandro Firmino da Hora as an adult), as well as the transformation of Cidade de Deus, to the late nineteen seventies. During this decade and a half, the *conjunto* changes from a poverty-stricken and crime-ridden neighbourhood to a literal war zone, where heavily-armed drug trafficking gangs battle for dominance in the absence of a corrupt and apathetic police service. Zé is one of the causes of this descent into anarchy, first provoking unnecessary conflict with one of his rivals, Carrot (played by Matheus Nachtergaele), and then arming the Runts, a gang of prepubescent children, as the conflict escalates. Rocket's growth takes a more conventional path and includes brief attempts to find legal employment and to pursue a criminal lifestyle until he discovers his passion for photography. In a manifold staging of poetic justice (see McGregor 2018b), Zé is murdered by the Runts and Rocket's capture of the murder on camera establishes his reputation as a photographer and secures his escape from the *conjunto*. The sequence in which the cinematic narrative represents these events is not completely linear, but is nonetheless easy to follow. What is more complicated is the narrative structure, which comprises numerous short narratives that coalesce into a complex narrative architecture to create multiple layers of meaning.

City of God is, as noted previously, the fictional autobiography of Rodrigues and the story of his escape from the deprivation and chaos of the *conjunto* to the creativity and fulfilment of life as a photographer in the city constitutes the overarching plot of the cinematic narrative (Diken and Laustsen 2007). The plot is divided into three parts of equal length by two crimes committed by Zé, who provides a counterpoint to Rocket (Rafter and Brown 2011): the revelation that he was the mass murderer in the brothel robbery (in the fortieth minute) and his rape of Ned's girlfriend (in the seventy-ninth minute). The revelation of the mass murder initiates Zé's rise to power in Cidade de Deus and the rape initiates the war with Ned (played by Seu Jorge) that causes the *conjunto's* descent into hyper-violent anarchy. *City of God* is unusual in that this overarching plot doesn't merely comprise one or more subplots, but is constituted by a conglomerate of three distinct levels of subplot, each of which is constituted by one or more narratives, each of which are explicitly identified as stories by means of either insert titles or Rocket's narration (or both). I shall call the overarching plot – the fictional autobiography – the primary story and the stories that constitute the descending layers of the narrative architecture secondary, tertiary, and quaternary respectively.

The intricacy of this architecture is compounded and confounded by the use of temporally asymmetric stories at the secondary, tertiary, and quaternary levels, where the stories vary in length from 92 minutes ('The Seventies', the longer of the two secondary stories) to no time at all (both of the quaternary stories). The secondary level divides the primary story into two parts, 'The Sixties' (which begins at 04:06) and 'The Seventies' (which begins at 32:42). 'The Sixties' comprises one tertiary story, 'The Story of the Tender Trio' (05:09), and two quaternary stories. I use *quaternary stories* to denote the tales that Rocket as narrator promises to tell, but that are never in fact represented on screen. The two quaternary stories in the secondary story of The Sixties are introduced as follows:

04:55   "But in order to tell Shaggy's story, I must tell the story of the Tender Trio" (*City of God* 2002).
14:38   "Shorty is another notorious guy in the City of God. But it is not yet time to tell his story" (*City of God* 2002).

The expectation that Shaggy (played by Jonathan Haagensen) and Shorty's (played by Gero Camilo) respective stories will be told in a similar manner to the other stories, identified by either insert titles or Rocket's narration, is frustrated as their stories dissolve into The Story of the Tender Trio. The longer of the two secondary stories, The Seventies, comprises seven tertiary stories, a structure that is complicated by self-reflexive narration and uncertainty as to whether there will be a quaternary story. The tertiary stories are told in the following order: 'The Story of the Apartment' (36:05), 'The Story of L'il Zé' (38:52), 'A Sucker's Life' (60:38), 'Flirting with Crime' (61:57), 'Benny's Farewell' (69:09), 'The Story of Knockout Ned' (87:57), and 'The Beginning of the End' (108:05).

The Seventies begins with a scene in which Rocket, Angélica (played by Alice Braga), and their friends go to the beach. Rocket agrees to buy Angélica cannabis and leaves the beach for the apartment of Blacky (played by Rubins Sabino), his former classmate. While Rocket is buying the cannabis, Zé arrives with several members of his gang and Rocket narrates The Story of the Apartment, which takes the narrative back in time. In a little over two minutes, the retrospective has caught up to the present and the audience once again sees Zé and his henchmen enter the apartment. The Story of the Apartment merges into The Story of L'il Zé, which also goes back in time, revealing Zé as the brothel murderer in the nineteen sixties and providing an overview of his rise to power as the most feared gangster in Cidade de Deus. The six-minute retrospective ends when the narrative once again returns to the scene in which Zé and his henchmen enter the apartment. At this point, it is unclear whether Rocket is narrating The Story of the Apartment, The Story of L'il Zé, or a third, untitled story that combines the two. Rocket fades into the background over the next 15 minutes, reasserting his narrative agency and refocusing the narrative on his autobiography with A Sucker's Life. Early in the next story, Flirting with Crime, Rocket meets Ned. During their initial conversation, the frame freezes on Ned's face for five seconds and Rocket narrates, "it's not time to tell Knockout Ned's story" (*City of God* 2002). Given that Shaggy and Shorty's promised stories never appeared, one cannot be sure as to whether Ned's will indeed be told and, in consequence, whether Ned is a significant character in the primary story. In this case, however, Rocket does fulfil his promise and The Story of Knockout Ned is crucial to the final third of the film, in which Cidade de Deus becomes the battlefield on which Ned and Zé wage their war against one another. The Beginning of the End returns to the opening scene of the film (the first four minutes), with Zé recruiting the Runts to his ranks by hosting a party at which he provides free food and firearms. Rocket initially fears he will be caught in a crossfire between Zé's gang and the police, but is then actually caught in a crossfire between Zé's gang and Ned's gang. Rocket demonstrates his courage and ingenuity in photographing both the firefight and its aftermath, which includes the murder of Zé by the Runts, and it is these photographs that facilitate his escape from Cidade de Deus.

The imposition of such a convoluted and elaborate narrative architecture on a relatively simple sequence of events replicates the multiplicity of intentions, desires, and fears that motivate the various members of the Cidade de Deus community. The self-reflexive narration foregrounds the fact that each resident in the *conjunto* is the protagonist of their own story, in consequence of which no one story can be enacted in isolation from the stories of others. The combination of narrative architecture with self-reflexive narration reproduces the way in which the multiple motivations of the characters overlap, intersect, and oppose one another to create a situation in which collaboration in or cooperation with organised crime are preferable to resistance. *City of God* employs this combination to represent the difficulty of resisting organised crime in both the real Cidade de Deus (in which it was still too dangerous to film two decades after the represented events) and in poverty-stricken, crime-ridden neighbourhoods more generally. It is important to note that the complex narrative architecture and self-reflexive storytelling in *City of God* do not collapse into a naïve psychological account of motivations for collaboration, cooperation, and resistance. Instead, the narrative fiction provides an account in which agency (psychological factors) is integrated with structure (socioeconomic factors) such that the everyday reality of the grip of organised criminal enterprises in neighbourhoods like Cidade de Deus is represented in detail and with accuracy. The film thus makes use of a combination of narrative devices to provide mimetic knowledge of the motivations for collaborating in, cooperating with, and resisting organised criminal enterprises. This knowledge consists of data that explains the obstacles to resisting organised crime and has criminological value to the extent that it could be used to weaken the influence of those enterprises in poverty-stricken and crime-ridden neighbourhoods.

Conclusion

I began this chapter by stating that there is a more robust relationship between the cinematic mode of representation and mimetic knowledge than between any of the other combinations of modes of representation and types of knowledge. I noted that mimesis has two denotations, the aesthetic, which is concerned with the re-creation of reality, and the anthropological, which is concerned with the imitation of reality. Mimetic knowledge is knowledge of everyday reality that is detailed and accurate and the mimetic value of a representation is the extent to which it provides such knowledge. The robust relation between the cinematic mode of representation and mimetic knowledge is in virtue of the mode's combined capacity for re-creation and imitation. I discussed re-creation in terms of characteristic realism, which I defined in terms of seven kinds of realism (content realism, photorealism, ontological realism, epistemic realism, perceptual realism, transparency, and anti-illusionism), arguing that the cinematic is the most realistic mode of representation. As such, the cinematic mode of representation has a greater potential for the detailed and accurate re-creation of everyday reality than, for example, the literary and the hybrid modes. I also claimed that the cinematic mode of representation has the potential for inducing mimicry, utilising the mechanism of evolutionary imitation to manipulate the emotions of audiences and, in consequence, has a greater potential for the imitation of everyday reality than the literary and hybrid modes. While the literary and hybrid modes of representation can provide mimetic knowledge, the strongest evidence of the provision of such knowledge by a narrative fiction will necessarily be found in cinematic narratives.

In order to demonstrate the mimetic element of the criminological value of narrative fiction, I therefore employed two cinematic narratives as case studies, *Miami Vice* (2006) and *City of God* (2002). In *Miami Vice*, Mann employs stylistic and structural devices to provide detailed and accurate knowledge of the absolute power wielded by the senior management of organised criminal enterprises. I explored the way in which this knowledge is provided by means of a detailed analysis of a particular scene in the film, which included a discussion of the relevance of its place within the overall narrative. In *City of God*, Meirelles and Lund employ a complicated narrative architecture and self-reflexive storytelling to provide detailed and accurate knowledge of the motivations for collaboration and cooperation with, and resistance to, organised criminal enterprises in deprived communities. I showed how the narrative architecture and self-reflexive narration reproduced the way in which the multiple motivations of the characters overlapped, intersected, and opposed one another to create a situation that impeded resistance to organised criminal enterprises. I also noted that there were various other ways in which the film could be considered as paradigmatic in providing mimetic knowledge, which included being a fictionalised autobiography, the use of amateur actors, and the location of the filming.

In each of the case studies, stylistic and narrative devices are employed to provide detailed and accurate knowledge of organised criminal enterprises, specifically the absolute power wielded by senior management and the obstacles to resisting organised crime. This mimetic knowledge constitutes the mimetic value of *Miami Vice* and *City of God* and the mimetic value is part and parcel of the works' respective criminological value in virtue of its aetiological character in each example. In both cases, the works provide mimetic knowledge that is not available to nonfictional representations for reasons of access, ethics, or law. The mimetic value of narrative fiction is not, of course, restricted to the particular knowledge I have articulated or to the two case studies I have employed, but can be found in many other exemplary narrative representations. Drawing on the examples I have used in this book so far, *No Country for Old Men*, *End of Watch*, *Prime Suspect*, and *Moby-Dick* are all obvious candidates for providing detailed and accurate knowledge of the everyday reality of crime and social harm. With my arguments for all of the phenomenological, counterfactual, and mimetic values of narrative fiction made, my argument for a criminology of narrative fiction is concluded. In the next chapter, I narrow my focus to the cinematic mode of representation, specifically to the phenomenon of the blockbuster feature film, in order to demonstrate the relationship between aetiological and pedagogic value within my criminology of narrative fiction.

7

Criminological Cinema

Introduction

In 'The ivorine tower in the city: Engaging urban studies after *The Wire*', Rowland Atkinson and David Beer (2010) argue that urban studies scholars, sociologists, and social scientists cannot afford to ignore the release of the fifth and final season of the HBO television series *The Wire* (2002–08) in 2008. Although they do not use the terms, they are concerned with both the aetiological and pedagogic values of the series: with the way in which the series provides knowledge of the city in late capitalist decline and with the way in which the series facilitates, augments, or enhances the communication of knowledge of the city in late capitalist decline. Atkinson and Beer offer a two-stage defence of *The Wire* as a paradigm-changing event in social science. First, they make the uncontroversial claim that the series meets the criteria for academic research, providing knowledge of the dynamics, inequities, and social problems characteristic of cities and exploring the possibilities for social progress in cities. This is *The Wire*'s aetiological value, which could also be expressed in terms of the capacity of the series to *do* urban studies. I (McGregor 2019) recently made a similar case for James Ellroy's (1995, 2001, 2009) *Underworld USA Trilogy*, arguing that the three novels taken together constitute a critical criminology because the *Trilogy* is an alternative way of doing criminology (an aspect of aetiological value that is related to, but distinct from, the provision of data that can be employed to reduce or prevent crime or social harm). I am thus in agreement that creating narrative fiction can be an alternative way of researching social science and my own experience of *The Wire* is sufficient to convince me that it is as valuable to criminology as it is to urban studies.

Having established that *The Wire* meets the criteria for academic research, Atkinson and Beer (2010) then claim that the five seasons taken together provide 60 hours of instruction on the city in late capitalist decline, divided into the following themes (like any academic module): drugs, gangs, and police; dock unions and city politics; city bureaucracy; education and social services; and news and the media machine. The reason that urban studies scholars ignore *The Wire* at

115

their peril is not because it is an alternative way of doing social science (aetiological value), but because as an alternative way of teaching social science it is self-evidently much more effective than the typical methods used in universities (pedagogic value). Atkinson and Beer describe this superiority as follows: 'a new kind of public urban sociology that generates a particular kind of training in the physics, forces and problems of the city' (2010: 532); 'the presence of ideas and issues we all work with that are now being more directly communicated to an audience without the apparent need for the formation of a second layer of meaning' (2010: 533); 'a kind of urban studies that bypasses many of the problems of communication often associated with academic work' (2010: 534); and 'an exemplary form of public social science' (2010: 534). The pedagogic value of the series is a function of the accessible manner in which it communicates ideas and issues to audiences and of the way in which audiences engage with the series as an extended exemplary narrative. If one had to deliver a module on the city in late capitalist decline as part of a degree programme, *The Wire* would thus not merely be able to provide the same knowledge, but to transfer that knowledge more successfully than even the most dynamic set of lectures, seminars, and tutorials. This pedagogic value is furthermore significant because of the size of the audience that the series has reached and will continue to reach. In other words, *The Wire* transfers the same knowledge more successfully and to a vastly bigger audience than any university module. In consequence, Atkinson and Beer identify two options for urban studies scholars: either 'piggy-back' on *The Wire*, using it as an aid to teaching (2010: 537); or 'eschew a focus upon novelty and identify long-term shifts and continuities' instead (2010: 538). The bulk of their article, which includes a brief discussion of *City of God* (2002), proposes a model in which research is focused on the long-term but more effort is made to disseminate research findings beyond the narrow confines of the academy.

I use Atkinson and Beer's article to introduce my concern in this chapter, the pedagogic value of narrative fiction, which is a departure from the previous three chapters, which have all been concerned with different elements of the aetiological value of narrative fiction. In Chapter 3, I noted that there were at least three distinct epistemic roles that narrative fictions could play in criminological inquiry: semiotic, pedagogic, and aetiological. The semiotic value of narrative fictions is in providing knowledge of the production and reception of representations of crime and its control. This role is characteristic of the cultural criminological framework. The pedagogic value of narrative fictions is in facilitating, augmenting, or enhancing the communication of knowledge of crime and its control. This role is characteristic of both the cultural criminological framework and the critical realist framework. I argued that, despite claims to the contrary, the critical realist frameworks deployed by Ruggiero (2003) and Frauley (2010) failed to fulfil the aetiological role, to provide knowledge of the causes of crime and social harm. In Chapters 4 to 6, I offered an argument for and evidence of the aetiological value of narrative fiction on the basis of the combination of the phenomenological, counterfactual, and mimetic knowledge provided by narrative fictions across different modes of representation. My aim was to establish that the aetiological role is characteristic of my criminology of narrative fiction. This aetiological value is not, however, incompatible with pedagogic value and in Chapter 3 I discussed the pedagogic value of *End of Watch* (2012). I have also employed several of the films whose aetiological value I have explored in this book – including *Cop Land* (1997), *Miami Vice* (2006), and *No Country for Old Men* (2007) – to augment my lecture and seminar delivery in a variety of undergraduate criminology modules. The purpose of this chapter is thus to establish the relationship between aetiological and pedagogic value within my criminology of narrative fiction.

My exploration of the pedagogic value of narrative fiction for criminology is focused exclusively on what I shall call *criminological cinema*: Hollywood feature films that take crime or social harm or the control of crime or social harm as their subject. I am not suggesting that narrative fictions in other modes of representation are lacking in pedagogic value, but my interest is in narrative fictions that reach audiences of dozens of millions, which necessarily limits me to either feature films produced in India, Nigeria, America, or China or television series produced in America (Motion Picture Association of America 2017; British Film Institute 2019). Following Atkinson and Beer (2010), I take pedagogic value as a function of accessible communication and audience engagement. My contention is that accessibility and engagement are themselves functions of the combination of the characteristic realism of the cinematic mode of representation and the mythic mode of storytelling. As mythic storytelling is more obvious in feature films than television series, my sketch of the pedagogic value of cinematic fictions is restricted to feature films. Finally, I limit my claims about criminological cinema to feature films produced in America by the Hollywood film industry on the basis that this industry and its productions will be the most familiar to the majority of my readers. I have no doubt that similar accounts could be constructed for the Indian, Nigerian, and Chinese film industries, but those accounts are better left to someone who is fluent in the respective languages and steeped in the respective cultures.

Popular criminology

In Chapter 6 I argued that the cinematic mode of representation has the greatest potential for mimetic value, for providing knowledge of the world by representing everyday reality in detail and with accuracy. This potential is in virtue of its characteristic realism, the extent to which cinematic representations appear to reproduce rather than represent reality. In consequence of this apparent reproduction, cinematic representations typically require minimal interpretation and are usually more accessible – more easily and more quickly understood – than hybrid or literary representations. Potential for providing detailed and accurate information is also potential for providing detailed and inaccurate misinformation and I noted in Chapter 3 that the cultural criminological engagement with cinematic representation had, aside from a few exceptions, been concerned with misrepresentation, with the confounding of the reality of crime and criminal justice with their own representations. The analysis of this misrepresentation in both fiction and nonfiction and narrative and non-narrative has made – and continues to make – a crucial contribution to criminology and I have no wish to marginalise that contribution here. My interest is in representation rather than misrepresentation, however, which aligns me more closely with the popular criminology pioneered by Philip Rawlings (1998), Michelle Brown (2004), and Nicole Rafter (2007b).

Rawlings (1998) identifies four types of criminological text: crime fiction, polemics, popular criminology, and academic criminology. He associates popular criminology with true crime writing and claims that the genre is standardly regarded with disdain by academic criminologists. Drawing on his own previous work (Rawlings 1992), Rawlings (1998: 10) makes the following case for the significance of popular criminology:

> The depiction of crime (fact and fiction) in books, newspapers, film, television and so forth has an impact on how crime is understood and, therefore, on policy, and this alone makes popular criminology worth studying. Leaving aside the possibility that popular criminologists may actually have something interesting to say about crime, there is the probability that they have a greater impact on policy than academics.

The probability he mentions is both a truism and worthy of attention because the readership of even the most renowned academic criminologists pales in comparison with the circulations of daily newspapers and the sales of popular crime novelists, let alone small and big screen audiences. For Rawlings, the combination of the fact that popular criminology is not necessarily misleading with the certainty of reaching a wider audience makes it worth taking seriously.

Brown (2004: 219) considers the relevance of popular culture to criminology and asks the pithy question, ' "What's in it" for criminology'? She briefly alludes to the pedagogic value of popular texts, but does not explore this subject until her collaboration with Rafter in their co-authored *Criminology Goes to the Movies: Crime Theory and Popular Culture* (Rafter and Brown 2011). In the interim, Rafter (2007b) published 'Crime, film and criminology: Recent sex-crime movies', which established popular criminology as a field of inquiry. The article argues for three related points: first that popular criminology is not only an aspect of criminology, but integral to the discipline; then that crime films are an aspect of popular criminology; and finally that film has criminological value in virtue of both the extent of its audience and in being able to 'bring to bear ethical, philosophical and psychological perspectives that are beyond the reach of academic research' (Rafter 2007b: 417). Rafter's position is not merely that popular criminology has criminological value, but that the discourse of popular criminology has greater social significance than the discourse of academic criminology. She defines *popular criminology* as:

> a category composed of discourses about crime found not only in film but also on the Internet, on television and in newspapers, novels and rap music and myth. Popular criminology differs from academic criminology in that it does not pretend to empirical accuracy or theoretical validity. But in scope, it covers as much territory – possibly more – if we consider the kinds of ethical and philosophical issues raised even by this small sample [six] of movies. Popular criminology's audience is bigger (even a cinematic flop will reach a larger audience than this article). And its social significance is greater, for academic criminology cannot offer so wide a range of criminological wares (Rafter 2007b: 415).

Rafter maintains that it is either no longer accurate or no longer desirable – she is not entirely clear on this point – that 'criminology' be regarded as referring to academic criminology because criminology is an umbrella term that includes the complementary discourses of popular criminology and academic criminology. It is also not entirely clear where popular criminology as a discourse fits in terms of the six levels of criminological inquiry I distinguished in Chapter 2. Framework, methodology, or theory seem the most likely candidates and while there is a sense in which popular criminology provides an alternative framework to cultural criminology, I think it is more accurately described as a methodology – a theory of research, a set of principles, and a system of methods regulating a particular inquiry – that is set out in greater detail and put to practical use in *Criminology Goes to the Movies*. Rafter and Brown (2011) begin by discussing the ways in which popular culture can augment criminology as a discipline, making contributions that academic criminology cannot, such as: speaking to diffuse cultural anxieties, shaping public opinion, and exploring the ways in which criminal behaviour is determined by values and emotions. They then narrow their concern to the relationship between crime film and crime theory and identify two ways in which crime film can contribute to crime theory. First, crime films are 'open texts', meaning that they are subject to multiple interpretations, in consequence of which a film as a text can incorporate multiple perspectives on crime, victimhood, and criminal justice (Rafter and Brown 2011: 8). Second, crime films can exploit their mode of representation – in particular, the technological and narrative elements – to explain the causes of crime in a manner that is 'better equipped' than academic criminology (Rafter and Brown 2011: 8).

In 'Living in the end times through popular culture: An ultra-realist analysis of *The Walking Dead* as popular criminology', Thomas Raymen (2018) cites Rafter's definition of popular criminology and divides the discourse into two categories.[1] Twentieth century popular criminology was focused on the ways in which crime was socially constructed and the ways in which crime, criminals, and the justice system were misrepresented (in other words, he regards popular criminology as continuous with, or employing the same framework as, cultural criminology). In contrast, twenty-first century popular criminology should be focused on confronting the 'disciplinary aetiological crisis', the construction of compelling theories of crime and social harm causation that can form the basis of crime and social harm reduction in practice (Raymen 2018: 432). Raymen does not specify whether he considers either Rafter (2007b) or Rafter and Brown (2011) to be engaged in the latter pursuit, but he describes Stephen Wakeman's (2018) work on violent entrepreneurialism in AMC's television series

Breaking Bad (2008–13) as exemplary. Raymen's own focus is on: the way in which Steve Hall's (2012) ultra-realist conceptions of pseudo-pacification, special liberty, and the criminal undertaker explain the violence in AMC's television series *The Walking Dead* (2010–19) and *Fear the Walking Dead* (2015–19); the relationship between the violence in the representations and violence in reality; and how the two series serve an ideological function in late capitalist society. Raymen's popular criminology project thus overlaps with my project in this book.

Rafter (2007b), Rafter and Brown (2011), and Raymen (2018) all draw attention to the significance of the relationship between popular culture and criminology and all argue that it is in some way reciprocal, with the representation of crime and social harm both influencing and being influenced by the reality of crime and social harm. They also all draw attention to the capacity of feature films and television series to represent rather than misrepresent and to reach large audiences. To this extent, I am entirely sympathetic. Rafter, Rafter and Brown, and Raymen also all make claims for the aetiological value of feature films and television series about which I am more sceptical. Rafter's (2007b) claim that crime films can reach beyond academic criminology to ethical, philosophical, and psychological perspectives seems to ignore the work of – to take just one example – Katz (1988), who achieves exactly this with *Seductions of Crime: Moral and Sensual Attractions in Doing Evil*. Similarly, I think Rafter and Brown's (2011: 2) claim that 'the encounter of theory with cinema is an engagement that leaves both fundamentally transformed' is disingenuous. In their preface, they explain that the book was motivated by their repeated discussion of two problems, both pedagogic: using films that students may not have seen as illustrations and improving knowledge retention beyond criminological theory modules. The aim of their book is clearly pedagogic rather than aetiological, 'making criminological theory comprehensible, engaging, and memorable' (Rafter and Brown 2011: x). Rafter and Brown succeed in this aim entirely, providing a model for teaching criminological theory that I have adopted in my own pedagogic practice, but they do not succeed in demonstrating that crime films explain the causes of crime as well as – let alone better than – academic criminology.[2]

Although Raymen (2018) acknowledges both the aetiological and pedagogic value of popular culture for criminology, he is clearly focused on aetiological value. He makes a convincing case for the various influences of reality (ultra-realist criminology and capitalist ideology) on representation, but his account of the influence of representation on reality is lacking in precision. This may well be a consequence of the article format in which Raymen's argument has been presented and I think he succeeds in sketching the foundation upon which a popular criminological framework – a shared commitment about what research questions are important, what data is relevant, how that data should be interpreted, and what counts as a satisfying answer – might be built in future. At present, however, popular criminology as practised by Rafter, Rafter and Brown, Raymen, and others has not provided a compelling argument for the aetiological value of popular cultural artefacts to criminology, in consequence of which popular criminology as a framework, methodology, or theory is distinct from my criminology of narrative fiction. Notwithstanding, there are two areas of overlap in the respective inquiries. First, there is a shared interest in popular culture, in that many (though not all) of the narrative fictions in which I am interested are popular cultural artefacts. Second, a shared interest in the *popular* in popular culture, in the significance of the size of the audience that popular cultural artefacts reach. The size of the audience determines the significance of the pedagogic value, which is why I have restricted my explanation of the pedagogic value of narrative fictions to criminological cinema. The pedagogic value is a function of accessible communication and audience engagement, which are in turn functions of the characteristic realism of the cinematic mode of representation and the mythic mode of storytelling employed by Hollywood.

Mythic storytelling

Aristotle (2004) famously offered a broad but useful definition of narrative, as a representation with a beginning, a middle, and an end. He was primarily concerned with the tragedies that formed such an important part of Greek culture and identified six constituents of a tragedy that determined its quality, the most important of which was plot (the others were character, diction, thought, spectacle, and song). Aristotle (2004: 1450a) defined a *tragedy* as 'the representation of an action that is complete and whole and of a certain magnitude' and *plot* as 'the ordered arrangement of the incidents'. The criterion for complete or whole representation was a plot with a recognisable beginning, middle, and end. Aristotle identified three pivotal elements of the plot: reversal, recognition, and suffering. The first two are more significant as they involve change, from a particular state of affairs to its opposite in reversal and from ignorance to knowledge in recognition. Aristotle maintained that the most effective recognition (anagnorisis) occurred when it was accompanied by a reversal of fortune (peripeteia). A contemporary example of this is David Fincher's *Seven* (1995), where Detective Mills' (played by Brad Pitt) anagnorisis that the sixth crime (motivated by the sin of envy) has already been perpetrated is accompanied by a peripeteia in which the victim of that crime is revealed to be his wife. In response, Mills murders John Doe (played by Kevin Spacey), completing Doe's planned series of seven crimes by enacting the sin of wrath in a conclusion that is as unexpected as it is dramatic. In the twenty-first century, Aristotle's beginning, middle, and end are more likely to be referred to as *exposition, complication,* and *resolution* respectively. To take the case study I shall employ in the next section as an example, Martin Brest's *Beverly Hills Cop* (1984) is 101 minutes long from beginning to end credits and has a readily discernible three-act structure: the exposition (first 19 minutes) begins with Detective Axel Foley's (played by Eddie Murphy) failed undercover operation and ends with his friend Mikey Tandino's (played by James Russo) murder; the complication begins with Foley's arrival in Beverly Hills and ends with him about to be murdered by Victor Maitland's (played by Steven Berkoff) henchmen; the resolution (last 20 minutes) begins with Detective Billy Rosewood's (played by Judge Reinhold) rescue of Foley and ends with the rescue of Foley's friend Jenny Summers (played by Lisa Eilbacher) and the death of Maitland.

The development of the three-act structure into the five acts popularised by Shakespeare has been traced back to the Roman poets Terence and Horace (Baldwin 1947). I refer to this movement from three to five acts as a development because it is an extrapolation of the three acts, specifically an extrapolation of the complication (Aristotle's middle) into three separate parts: *rising action, climax,* and *crisis* (Freytag 1894). To return to *Beverly Hills Cop*, the exposition and resolution remain the same (roughly the first and last 20 minutes of the film), but the complication (the hour in the middle) is structured in more detail, as follows: the rising action begins when Foley arrives in Beverly Hills and ends when he identifies Maitland as a suspect in Tandino's murder (at 30 minutes); the climax begins with Foley being arrested and meeting Rosewood, Sergeant John Taggart (played by John Ashton), and Lieutenant Andrew Bogomil (played by Ronny Cox) and ends with Foley being arrested a second time (at 66 minutes); the crisis begins with Bogomil taking Foley's allegations against Maitland seriously and ends with Foley about to be murdered (at 81 minutes).

A decade after the unprecedented commercial success of Steven Spielberg's *Jaws* in 1975, a Disney screenwriter named Christopher Vogler wrote a memorandum in which he identified the structure of *Jaws* and subsequent Hollywood blockbusters like George Lucas' *Star Wars Trilogy* (1977, 1980, 1983; now known as the *Original Trilogy*) and

Spielberg's *E. T. the Extra-Terrestrial* (1982) as following the monomyth established by Joseph Campbell (1949) in *The Hero with a Thousand Faces*. Campbell's book was a work of comparative mythology in which he drew on the ideas of Carl Gustav Jung, Friedrich Nietzsche, Adolf Bastian, Franz Boas, James G. Frazer, and Sigmund Freud to propose a monomyth or universal archetype upon which all global myths and legends were based. Campbell (1949: 57) called this universal archetype the 'hero-journey' and divided it into three stages: departure, initiation, and return. John Yorke (2013: 54) summarises this archetypal story as: 'A hero ventures forth from the world of common day into a region of supernatural wonder: fabulous forces are there encountered and a decisive victory is won: the hero comes back from this mysterious adventure with the power to bestow boons on his fellow man.' In Vogler's memorandum, which was subsequently expanded to book length and published as *The Writer's Journey: Mythic Structure for Storytellers and Screenwriters* (1992), he distilled Campbell's monomyth into a simple formula, a design consisting of twelve stages divided into five acts. Yorke (2013) provides an analysis of Vogler's model and argues that an overwhelming majority of commercially successful films have followed the model exactly, proceeding through each of the twelve stages by means of five parts. In other words, there is something about this mode of storytelling – he suggests a complex combination of features in the final chapter of his book – that resonates with human beings no matter what their spatiotemporal location. Yorke cites dozens of examples of feature films that follow the model, but the match with *Jaws* is the closest, which is to be expected given that it is widely acknowledged as the first 'event movie', 'tent pole picture' or 'summer blockbuster' (Shone 2004: 28 and 37).[3] Tom Shone (2004) goes as far as to claim that the Hollywood film industry remodelled itself in the image of *Jaws* from the mid-nineteen seventies and mentions *Beverly Hills Cop* as one of the products of this remodelling.

Yorke (2013) superimposes the following template on the five-act structure: call to action, initial objective achieved, the point of no return, all is lost (or won), and resolution in victory (or defeat). The call to action is what motivates the protagonist to change the routine of her life by pursuing a particular goal; for example, the murder of Tandino motivates Foley to find his killer, in the course of which he leaves Detroit for Beverly Hills. Relatively quickly, an initial objective is achieved; for example, Foley identifies Maitland as a suspect in the murder and the film suggests that Maitland will be (at least one of) the main antagonist(s) as the story unfolds. The point of no return occurs in the third act and Yorke holds that it is almost always timed to the precise halfway point in popular film; for example, in the fifty-first minute (50:45 of 101 minutes), Foley tells Taggart and Rosewood, "We're cops, we should be working together" (*Beverly Hills Cop* 1984) and from this point onwards Foley is assisted by Rosewood, Taggart, and Bogomil in various combinations and in various ways. The point of no return or turning point is the point at which the resolution of the film becomes inevitable and the story of *Beverly Hills Cop* is the story of Foley – the unorthodox, street-smart cop from Detroit – becoming a Beverly Hills cop: working with rather than against his orthodox, procedure-bound, Californian counterparts. The turning point is also the point in the narrative where there is a change in storytelling, from the story being driven by what the hero wants to the story being driven by what the hero needs, by the hero being forced to overcome a character flaw or vice and, in so doing, achieving some kind of psychological self-actualisation (this process – like the *all is lost* below – can be reversed, in tragedies where the psychological transformation proceeds from virtue to vice). What Foley wants is to bring Tandino's murderer to justice, but what he needs is to learn to work with others, whether those others are colleagues in Detroit or in Beverly Hills. As soon as Taggart and Rosewood befriend Foley, Foley is firmly set on the path of becoming a team player, to being accepted by Bogomil and even, with reluctance, by Chief Hubbard (played by Stephen Elliott), head of the Beverly Hills Police Department (BHPD).

At some stage during the fourth act, usually at its end, the story reaches a point where it either appears that all is lost and the protagonist is certain to fail to achieve their goal (if the story ends in victory) or where it appears that all is won and the protagonist is certain to succeed in achieving their goal (if the story ends in defeat). *Beverly Hills Cop* is an example of the former (which is much more common) and all appears lost when Foley and Jenny are captured by Maitland, who orders his henchmen to take Jenny to his house and to kill Foley (80 minutes in to the film). Resolution can involve either victory or defeat and is either a reversal of the all is lost situation or a reversal of the all is won situation. This reversal is often subdivided into separate parts; for example, there is a carefully-staged crescendo of action in *Beverly Hills Cop*, where the last 20 minutes involve first Rosewood's rescue of Foley (81 minutes), then Taggart's decision to join Rosewood and Foley (84 minutes), and finally Bogomil's decision to join Taggart, Rosewood, and Foley (89 minutes). In the final action sequence of the film both Foley and Bogomil shoot Maitland dead. This is important in drawing attention to Foley's psychological development, from lying to his inspector in Detroit to jointly avenging Tandino with the lieutenant in Beverly Hills. When Bogomil takes responsibility for the presence of Taggart, Rosewood, and Foley on Maitland's property, Hubbard reluctantly endorses the police operation and the story has reached its conclusion with Foley a Beverly Hills cop, working for Bogomil with Hubbard's approval.

Beverly Hills Cop is thus an example of Campbell's monomyth, an instantiation of the archetypal story in which a hero (Foley) ventures forth from the world of common day (Detroit) into a region of supernatural wonder (Beverly Hills): fabulous forces (Maitland and his henchmen) are there encountered and a decisive victory is won: the hero comes back from this mysterious adventure (avenging Tandino's murder) with the power (transformation into a team player) to bestow boons on his fellow man. Recall from my discussions of *The Wire* and popular criminology that pedagogic value is constituted by a combination of accessible communication and audience engagement. The characteristic realism of the cinematic mode of representation facilitates accessible communication, but it also contributes to audience engagement. Unlike literary and hybrid representations, feature films engage audiences on two sensory levels, visual and audial, and the experience of watching a film is in consequence more immersive than that of reading a novel or graphic novel. The mythic mode of storytelling similarly contributes to both audience engagement and accessible communication. There is something about this particular way of telling a story that enhances audience engagement and Shone (2004) characterises the blockbuster in terms of the combination of audience participation (people talking about the film and buying related merchandise) and a relatively high proportion of repeat viewings. It is because these films employ the mythic mode of storytelling that they are so popular. This mode of storytelling also contributes to accessible communication, however, because the structure it employs is one with which all audiences are familiar, from their earliest memories of bedtime stories to watching Disney films as children to watching crime films as adults. With regard to narrative form, we know what to expect when we watch a Hollywood feature film, which makes it easier to follow the substantive details represented. The combination of the characteristic realism of the cinematic mode of representation and the mythic mode of storytelling in Hollywood feature films thus contributes to the accessible communication and the audience engagement that constitute the pedagogic value of criminological cinema. This combination is the mechanism by means of which criminological cinema facilitates, augments, or enhances the communication of knowledge of crime and its control. As I noted in Chapter 3, the claim that cinematic narratives have pedagogic potential is not controversial; what is controversial is the significance of that pedagogic potential.

Beverly Hills Cop

Beverly Hills Cop (1984) was a commercial success, earning over twenty times what it cost to make in ticket sales alone (Nash Information Services 2019). The film dominated the box office in the US for thirteen consecutive weeks following its release on 5 December 1984 and was the highest-grossing film in the US that year (IMDB 2019a). If one uses the Box Office Mojo ticket price adjuster, this gross translates to just under 70 million theatre tickets sold in the US (Nash Information Services 2019). A proportion of the audience would no doubt have seen the film twice and a proportion of repeat reviewers seen it multiple times. Even allowing for 25 million repeat viewings (roughly a third of ticket sales), 45 million people in the US watched *Beverly Hills Cop* in movie theatres in 1984 and 1985, which was almost a fifth of the population of the country (Bureau of the Census 1984). After adjusting for inflation, *Beverly Hills Cop* is the forty-seventh most successful film at the US box office to date (IMDB 2019b). The international audience of the film on initial release was approximately a third of the US audience in size, but the number of people who have watched the film in the last three and a half decades would have increased exponentially due to its release on video, television, DVD, Blu-ray, and streaming services (IMDB 2019a). At the time of writing, both the film and its two sequels (1987, 1994) are readily available on DVD, Blu-ray, and numerous streaming services. There is only one other crime film in the list of the top one hundred most successful films at the US box office, Francis Ford Coppola's *The Godfather* (1972), which is twenty-sixth on the list, sold approximately 10 million more tickets, and cost less to make than *Beverly Hills Cop*. I have selected *Beverly Hills Cop* on the basis that, unlike *The Godfather*, its reputation was established by its commercial rather than critical success. There seems little doubt that hundreds of millions of people have engaged with the film, but the relevant question is whether those hundreds of millions are likely to have come away from the experience any the wiser to crime and its control, that is whether a feature film that is a popular success but has attracted little or no serious, critical, or sociological attention can have significant pedagogic value for criminology.

There are a couple of things that immediately strike one on watching (or in my case, re-watching) the film nearly four decades after its release. The first is that unlike so many films from the eighties, it has aged remarkably well, remaining funny (very funny, in my opinion) and achieving its humour for the most part inoffensively. Yes, there is some regrettable homophobia from Foley and the only woman represented is Jenny, who plays a completely passive role. The homophobia is nonetheless implicit rather than explicit and while Jenny has little impact on the plot aside from requiring rescue in the resolution she is at least depicted as a success story, having transcended her humble origins with Foley and Tandino in Detroit by joining the social elite in Beverly Hills. Murphy has several great lines as Foley, which he delivers with typical confidence and charisma and Rosewood, Taggart, and Bogomil provide a trio of straight men to offset his role as the comedian. The opening scene, a thrilling but realistic police chase that Foley spends trying to avoid being thrown out the back of an articulated lorry – all to the sound of The Pointer Sisters' 'Neutron Dance' (Willis and Sembello 1984) – very much sets the tone for the rest of the film: it is exciting, fast-paced, funny, and establishes Foley as a talented but maverick detective who prefers to work alone. The comedy intensifies once Foley arrives in Beverly Hills because Brest exaggerates the contrast between Beverly Hills, the BHPD, and Rosewood, Taggart, and Bogomil on the one hand and Detroit, the Detroit Police Department, and Foley on the other hand. The Beverly Hills detectives all wear suits and follow police procedure and the letter of the law. Foley has already been introduced as a talented maverick and he always dresses casually – a sweatshirt, jeans, and sneakers, with a tracksuit top for special occasions. The differences in police culture are set out in Bogomil's first exchange with Foley, which follows Foley's assault by Taggart (*Beverly Hills Cop* 1984):

Bogomil: Detective Foley, I'm Lieutenant Bogomil of the Beverly Hills Police Department. Do you wish to file charges against Sergeant Taggart?

Foley: This is some kind of joke, right?

Bogomil: Do you wish to file charges against this officer for assault?

Foley: Look, where I'm from cops don't file charges against other cops. No, I don't wanna do that.

Bogomil: Well in Beverly Hills we go strictly by the book.

The visual disparity between Foley and Rosewood, Taggart, and Bogomil is emphasised by the amalgamation of acting, *mise-en-scène*, and cinematography. Foley is dressed scruffily and seated for most of the scene. The BHPD detectives all wear two- or three-piece suits, are all taller than Murphy, and all stand for most or all of the scene. They are also all white and the three tall, smart, white men could not present more of a contrast with the scruffy, black man of medium height.

And this is the second thing that strikes one on watching the film now – that despite ethnicity being used to establish the contrast between comedian and straight men and Detroit and Beverly Hills, Foley experiences no explicit racism in the film, not even from the (all-white) villains. This is a directorial choice by Brest, which seems likely to have been made for a combination of commercial and artistic reasons. With respect to commerce, had Foley problematised his blackness, a proportion of the white audience would probably have been alienated. With respect to art, the representation of racism would have detracted from the humour of the film – had Foley been subjected to racial slurs, for example, it would have been difficult to maintain the light-hearted, upbeat narrative tone. Another way of putting this would be that Brest chose to avoid or subdue any serious, sociological, or criminological content in order to engage a wider audience, maximise profit, or both. As such, *Beverly Hills Cop* is an unlikely example of criminological cinema, reaching a mass audience but apparently failing to communicate anything of criminological significance to that audience. Throughout the film there are only two references to ethnicity, one explicit and one implicit, both made by Foley himself. The first is when Foley bluffs his way into one of Maitland's warehouses and impersonates a customs officer. He asks the manager, "How can a black man, dressed like me, just march into your warehouse, walk into the bonded area, without anyone asking me any questions whatsoever?" (*Beverly Hills Cop* 1984). Shortly after, when Bogomil has assigned two new detectives, Foster (played by Art Kimbro) and McCabe (played by Joel Bailey), to follow Foley, Foley ridicules Foster's accent and diction, telling him that he has been spending too much time with McCabe. The implication is that Foster (who is black) has allowed himself to be assimilated by the white American culture of the BHPD, represented in this scene by McCabe (who is white). These two casual references to ethnicity seem to be all the film has to say on the subject – too little to be of interest to the criminologist. The reason I have selected *Beverly Hills Cop* as my final case study, however, is that in spite of sacrificing criminological content for popular appeal it succeeds in facilitating the communication of knowledge of intersectionality.

Intersectionality has a complex history, but is usually associated with one or more of the black feminism of the Combahee River Collective (1977), the critical race theory of Kimberlé Williams Crenshaw (1989), or the feminist sociology of Regina Arnold (1990). Hillary Potter

(2015: 3) defines it as: 'the concept or conceptualization that each person has an assortment of coalesced socially constructed identities that are ordered into an inequitable social stratum.' In *Beverly Hills Cop*, the relevant socially constructed identities are socioeconomic status and ethnicity. Socioeconomic status is explored not just in terms of wealth, but also what Pierre Bourdieu (1984) refers to as *cultural capital*, which combines personal preferences with level of education and status of social origin to provide an indication of competence in negotiating the cultural economy. While the contrast between Foley and his BHPD colleagues is exploited for comedy, the contrast between Foley and Maitland is exploited for exploring intersectionality. Where Foley is a (relatively) poor black detective who uses colloquial language, dresses scruffily, has popular tastes, and lives in a flat in Detroit, Maitland is a wealthy white businessman who is impeccably-dressed, well-spoken (his accent is non-regional British English, exaggerating the contrast), owns an art gallery, and lives in a mansion in Beverly Hills. The reluctance of Taggart, Bogomil, and Hubbard to take Foley's allegations against Maitland seriously is based on Maitland's socioeconomic status: on the power he can exert through his wealth, the legal consequences that would follow libellous accusations or false arrest, and his standing in the Beverly Hills community.

To the differential established by socioeconomic status, which is explicit (Maitland's cultural capital and power are revealed to the audience and discussed by characters in the film), Brest adds ethnicity, which is implicit. The intersection of socioeconomic status with ethnicity that defines Foley places him on the wrong side of inequality in Beverly Hills. As a black cop from Detroit, he is disadvantaged to a greater extent than the (mostly) white cops from Beverly Hills, who in turn lack the advantage and influence of the wealthy, white businessman from Beverly Hills. This is what Foley is referring to when he says *a black man, dressed like me*. In the scene in which he makes this comment, he is impersonating a customs officer and chastising the warehouse manager for security so ineffectual that a black male of apparently low socioeconomic status can gain access to the premises without being challenged. The implication is that Foley and the warehouse staff are all well aware that the security measures in place are precisely aimed at keeping poor, black men out. The conversation begins in the forty-eighth minute of the film, in between the two occasions on which Foley is arrested. The warehouse scene, which is the only time in the whole film that Foley mentions his ethnicity and the cumulative effects of ethnic and socioeconomic disadvantage, is followed by the turning point in the narrative, where Foley, Taggart, and Rosewood work together to foil an armed robbery. Brest thus raises the issue of intersectional disadvantage and then immediately places Taggart and Rosewood on the side of the disadvantaged Foley. There is a reminder of the ethnic element of cumulative disadvantage in Foley's conversation with Foster (in the sixtieth minute of the film) before Bogomil joins Taggart and Rosewood in support of Foley (in the sixty-eighth minute of the film). Even though the ethnic element of intersectionality has been deliberately (and irresponsibly, in my opinion) subdued by Brest, the quick succession of Foley's explicit and implicit references to ethnicity draws the audience's attention to the way in which black ethnicity combines with low socioeconomic status to multiply disadvantage.

I am not suggesting that *Beverly Hills Cop* has aetiological value, like *City of God* (2002) or *Miami Vice* (2006), or even that it has equivalent pedagogic value to *End of Watch* (2012), *Cop Land* (1997), or *No Country for Old Men* (2007). On the contrary, I have been clear that Brest sacrificed potential pedagogic value to reach as wide an audience as possible, to keep that audience laughing, and to encourage part of that audience to watch the film again on the big screen, small screen, or both. The film nonetheless facilitates the communication of some criminological knowledge, suggesting that certain groups in society suffer the consequences of cumulative disadvantages (the Foleys), in contrast to other groups that enjoy cumulative advantages (the Maitlands). Granted, the exploration of intersectionality in the film is limited and unsophisticated, but it could nonetheless be put to pedagogic use in the classroom. One can imagine, for example, being asked what intersectionality is by a student and answering by asking the class why Foley was thrown through a window and punched, why he was able to convince the warehouse manager that there had been a major security breach, and why Hubbard was so reluctant to investigate Maitland. A discussion would quickly reveal that the answers involved not just socioeconomic status but also ethnicity – that intersectionality plays a role in determining one's relationship with the criminal justice system. One might regard this as a minor, perhaps even trivial, facilitation of knowledge about intersectionality, but one must balance the lack of complexity against the mass audience the knowledge has reached.

Conclusion

I began this chapter with a discussion of Atkinson and Beer's (2010) article on the significance of *The Wire* (2002–08) for urban studies, a significance based on the combination of both aetiological and pedagogic values. I focused on pedagogic value, described by Atkinson and Beer as a function of accessible communication and audience engagement. I identified my interest in the pedagogic value of narrative fiction as being restricted to criminological cinema, to Hollywood feature films that take crime or social harm or the control of crime or social harm as their subject. I proposed that the accessible communication by and audience engagement with these cinematic representations is a function of the characteristic realism of the cinematic mode of representation and the mythic mode of storytelling. As I had already explained characteristic realism in Chapter 6, I proceeded directly to mythic storytelling, which I illustrated using *Beverly Hills Cop* (1984). I suggested that the film is very likely the second most-watched crime film of all time (after *The Godfather*), but nonetheless an unlikely example of popular criminology given that Brest appears to have sacrificed the *criminology* in 'popular criminology' for the sake of the *popular*. I demonstrated that despite subduing criminological and sociological content – specifically, the representation of racism – the cinematic narrative has pedagogic value in facilitating the communication of knowledge about intersectionality.

While the exploration of intersectionality is limited and unsophisticated, it has reached a mass audience across the globe, in consequence of which it should not be ignored by criminologists. Brest's exploration of intersectionality may even be trivial, but the crucial point is that he represents rather than misrepresents the concept. At worst, the film thus fails to communicate anything of criminological significance about intersectionality (rather than actively misinforming the audience). I drew attention to several scenes in a twenty-odd minute section of the film (47:21 to 68:50) and argued that their juxtaposition provided some exploration of both the ethnic and socioeconomic elements of intersectionality. I then provided an example of how even this limited and unsophisticated exploration might be incorporated into pedagogic practice. At the time of writing, I teach the second year module ' "Race", Crime and Criminology', the second half of which is exclusively focused on intersectionality. Were *Beverly Hills Cop* recent enough to have been watched by the majority of my students (most of whom are aged 19–21), it would make for an excellent introduction to – and a way of stimulating classroom discussion of – the concept, which we naturally probe in much more depth than the film. At present, I use a seven-minute YouTube clip by Kat Blaque (2019), which is excellent, but not quite as accessible or as engaging as a Hollywood feature film. My point is that if even a film that has attracted no criminological attention and sacrificed the critical to the commercial has pedagogic value for criminology, then criminological cinema should be taken seriously by criminologists.

In other words, I am endorsing the claims that Rafter, Rafter and Brown, Raymen, and other popular criminologists make about the pedagogic value of popular culture. This comment by Dimitros Akrivos and Alexandros Antoniou (2019: 335–36) summarises my view of *Beverly Hills Cop* in particular and criminological cinema in general:

> popular criminology is not (neither does it aspire to be) as theoretically grounded or empirically evidenced as academic criminology but can actually have a much greater cultural impact than the latter, as it goes beyond the academic community and has the potential to reach a far higher number of people ...

Beverly Hills Cop facilitates the communication of a superficial but broadly accurate conception of intersectionality to an audience of millions of people each year whereas my ' "Race", Crime and Criminology' module transfers knowledge of a sophisticated conception of intersectionality to 15–25 students each year. Popular criminology and academic criminology are both important to the discipline of criminology. My criminology of narrative fiction is not only compatible with recognising the pedagogic value of popular cultural artefacts, but encourages criminologists to engage with popular fictions. To my mind, it is something that we do not do enough of and are far too quick to dismiss when we see others doing it. Having established the aetiological value narrative fiction by arguing for the phenomenological, counterfactual, and mimetic values of narrative fiction and identified the pedagogic value of narrative fiction as complementary to this aetiological value, I am now in a position to summarise my case for a criminology of narrative fiction.

8

Conclusion: Criminology of Narrative Fiction

The Departed

I have used seven case studies in this book, the first six to demonstrate the aetiological value of narrative fiction for criminology and the seventh to demonstrate the pedagogic value of narrative fiction for criminology. My weighting among these case studies reveals my primary interest in narrative fiction from a criminological perspective, which is in the cinematic mode of representation in general and feature films in particular. As discussed in Chapter 7, my focus has been on the Hollywood film industry and within that industry, for obvious reasons, on the genre of crime films. Within that genre, I have nonetheless neglected the single most famous director, Martin Scorsese. Scorsese has directed *Taxi Driver* (1976), *Goodfellas* (1990), *Casino* (1995), and many other critically and commercially successful films, but did not win the Oscar for Best Director until *The Departed* in 2006. *The Departed* is a remake of Andrew Lau and Alan Mak's much-lauded *Infernal Affairs* (2002), a product of the Hong Kong film industry. Scorsese tells the story of two young Irish American men growing up in precarious circumstances in a deprived part of South Boston. Colin Sullivan (played by Matt Damon) is groomed by crime boss Frank Costello (played by Jack Nicholson), who persuades him to join the Massachusetts State Police (MSP) as a spy for Costello's organised criminal enterprise. Several years later, Billy Costigan (played by Leonardo DiCaprio) is recruited direct from the police academy by Captain Queenan (played by Martin Sheen) to join Costello's enterprise as an undercover officer. In order to maintain operational security, Costigan will be dismissed from the MSP during his initial training, with only Queenan and his deputy in the Undercover Section, Staff Sergeant Dignam (played by Mark Wahlberg), privy to the information that Costigan is still a police officer, on a covert operation. The drama, pace, and tension of the narrative fiction are all underpinned by the comparison and contrast of Costigan with Sullivan and the attempts of each to discover the identity of the other – beginning with Sullivan's promotion to detective in the Special Investigation Unit (SIU), the MSP's organised crime task force, which is coincidental with Costigan's recruitment by Queenan.

My case studies all isolated a particular aetiological value in a particular narrative fiction (for example, counterfactual value in *Broadchurch 3* and mimetic value in *City of God*) for the purpose of demonstrating the ways in which different types of knowledge are provided by different modes of representation. In practice, however, it is much more common for a particular narrative fiction to provide two or even all three types of knowledge at the same time and *The Departed* is a paradigmatic example. I noted that the drama, pace, and tension of the film are all driven by the juxtaposition of Costigan and Sullivan. As the narrative progresses, Costigan emerges as the protagonist and the stakes are raised when the very circumstances that protect him – his anonymity – make him vulnerable to both Costello and the MSP. Courtesy of Sullivan's efforts, Queenan is killed by Costello's men, in consequence of which the loyal but volatile Dignam resigns. This leaves Costigan completely isolated – neither an undercover officer nor a committed criminal – and makes Sullivan's task of finding him easier. As is often the case in fictional representations, it is precisely when the narrative seems to be on the verge of failing to suspend disbelief that it is at its most realistic, providing detailed and accurate knowledge of the everyday reality of covert operations. Undercover policing has always been fraught with moral, legal, and political pitfalls, as has been the use of confidential informants (Harfield and Harfield 2018). The protection of the identity of undercover officers and confidential informants is crucial to the success of covert investigations and there have been frequent historical cases where confusion within the police or security services (or between the police and the security services) has resulted in the preventable loss of life. Two examples from my own research and teaching spring to mind immediately: the unsolved murder of Anton Lubowski during the last-ditch defence of apartheid by the Civil Cooperation Bureau in Namibia in 1989 (McGregor 2018b) and the Metropolitan Police Service's mismanagement of Yardie informants in London in the early nineties (Murji 1996).

To this self-defeating level of secrecy, *The Departed* adds the interdepartmental competition within the police, between Queenan's Undercover Section and Captain Ellerby's (played by Alec Baldwin) SIU. The rivalry is used by Scorsese as a vehicle for comedy, as in the following exchange among Dignam, Ellerby, and FBI Special Agent Lazio (played by Robert Wahlberg) during a SIU briefing:

Lazio:	Without asking for too many details, do you have anyone in with Costello presently?
Dignam:	Maybe, maybe not, maybe fuck yourself. My theory on Feds is they're like mushrooms: feed 'em shit and keep 'em in the dark. You girls have a good day.
Ellerby:	Normally he's a very … er … nice guy. Don't judge him from this meeting alone. (*The Departed* 2006)[1]

The humorous representation of the (un)friendly rivalry conceals a problematic clash of strong personalities, which recalls *The Wire's* (2002–2008) representation of police units and agencies working at cross-purposes and, in doing so, facilitating rather than reducing crime and social harm. In *The Departed*, the inter-departmental rivalry and personality clashes have fatal consequences for Costigan following Dignam's resignation in protest against the SIU's failure to prevent Queenan's murder.

Costigan is the protagonist to Sullivan's antagonist and has the most to lose should he be exposed: where the discovery of Sullivan's links to Costello would result in arrest and incarceration, the discovery of Costigan's identity as a police officer would result in him being tortured to death by Costello. By employing Costigan as his protagonist and using an initial close comparison with Sullivan that gradually gives way to complete contrast, Scorsese provides knowledge of the lived experience of working undercover, focusing on the effects of living with the continuous threat of death by torture and of maintaining two distinct personalities over an extended period of time. *The Departed* also draws attention to the impossibility of forming meaningful and sincere relationships at the time when they are most needed. Costigan has a brief affair with his psychiatric parole supervisor, Madolyn Madden (played by Vera Farmiga), who – in a further complication of juxtaposition and escalation of suspense – is living with Sullivan. Costigan's deteriorating mental health is demonstrated by his increasing instability and his growing reliance on opioids, benzodiazepines, and alcohol to maintain the semblance of calm. Rafter (2007a) regards the mistrust, corruption, and confusion at the heart of *The Departed* as political commentary on America post-9/11, under the Bush administration. Making a case for this interpretation would require more evidence than she provides in her blog post, but whatever metaphorical role the mistrust, corruption, and confusion play, they raise the phenomenological value of *The Departed* to an approximation of Mike Newell's *Donnie Brasco* (1997), which provides the most comprehensive and compelling phenomenological knowledge of the lived experience of undercover policing that I have ever seen onscreen.

Finally, *The Departed* provides knowledge of reality by exploring alternatives to that reality – foregrounding the threat posed by agents of organised crime in and to policing. This danger is acute, particularly when one considers the vast financial resources (and accompanying power) available to transnational organised crime enterprises and the pressure on police services worldwide to democratise their respective workforces by recruiting from the communities they police (Wainwright 2016; Manning 2010). The numerous advantages of having an undercover operative in the police as opposed to relying on corrupt police officers are explored in more detail across all five (to date) seasons of the BBC's *Line of Duty* (2012–19) television series. Like Sullivan in *The Departed*, Detective Inspector Matthew Cottan (played by Craig Parkinson) rises to a position where he is particularly useful to the organised criminal enterprise for which he works (AC-12, the fictional police service's anti-corruption unit). When Cottan is killed, his boss exploits the well-intentioned efforts of Constable Simon Bannerjee (played by Neet Mohan) to divert Ryan Pilkington (played by Gregory Piper) from a life of crime to have Pilkington replace Cottan. The two most obvious advantages to organised criminal enterprises of having someone like Sullivan in the police are both related to risk. First, the chances of Sullivan betraying Costello are reduced given that Costello has been priming him for the role since childhood. Second, the danger period is during recruitment and selection – when Sullivan's criminal record and background are being scrutinised – rather than when he is actually passing information to Costello. Were Costello to rely on corrupt police officers, they would be both more likely to betray him and more likely to be detected. As such, *The Departed* has aetiological value in virtue of the mimetic, phenomenological, and counterfactual knowledge it provides. This criminological knowledge consists of data that explains the vulnerability of the police to organised criminal enterprises and could be used to improve police policy, procedure, and practice.

Narrative criminologies

Narrative criminology was established by Lois Presser (2008, 2009, 2013, 2018), who remains the leading voice in the field. Narrative criminology is most accurately described as a framework for criminological inquiry and can be characterised in terms of:

(1) a realist approach to social reality, which assumes the social world is an external reality and that social facts have a truth value, but that researchers have only partial access to the truth;

(2) core commitments to: (a) story as one of the main explanatory variables in criminology; (b) the relevance of stories to the causes of crime and social harm; and (c) the relevance of stories to desistance from crime and social harm;

(3) an emphasis on narrative form (genre, structure, function, and framework) as opposed to narrative content (subject, theme, characters, settings, and actions);

(4) a focus on life stories and the way in which they construct personal identity;

(5) a constitutive approach to the relationship between narrative and reality, in which narratives have a reciprocal relationship with experience such that they both produce experience and are the products of experience; and

(6) attention to the significance of the relationship between narrative and ethical value on the one hand and life stories and moral selfhood on the other hand.

My criminology of narrative fiction shares the realist approach to social reality with the narrative criminological framework (1) as well as all three of the framework's core commitments: exemplary narratives are significant to the discipline of criminology; exemplary narratives have aetiological value; and exemplary narratives contribute to desistance (2). I also share Presser's emphasis on narrative form, although my emphasis is on both narrative form *and* narrative content – specifically, on the ways in which their integration can provide different types of knowledge across different modes of representation – rather than narrative form at the expense of narrative content (3). As its name suggests, my criminology of narrative fiction is concerned exclusively with exemplary narratives that are fictional, where fiction is understood as a practice in which representations are both produced and experienced as fictions and in which there is an expectation of (and tolerance for) invention, imagination, and fabrication (4). My interest in these exemplary narratives is the extent to which (and ways in which) they represent rather than misrepresent reality, that is with a representational relationship between narrative and reality (5). In contrast, Presser's concern is with life stories and although these stories are regarded as having a constitutive relation with reality (to which the categories of 'fiction' and 'nonfiction' are irrelevant), the focus of narrative criminology to date has been almost exclusively on nonfictional narratives. Where Presser makes extensive use of the ethical value of narratives in her discussions of the heroic struggle, cultural logics, and moral emotions, the relationship between narrative representation and ethical value that I explored in *Narrative Justice* (McGregor 2018b) has no role in my criminology of narrative fiction (6).

On the basis that the similarities between my theory and Presser's framework (1–3) are more significant than the differences (4–6), my criminology of narrative fiction is most accurately described as emergent from the narrative criminological framework.

Fictional criminologies

Jon Frauley's (2010) theory of fictional realities, which focuses on feature films providing empirical referents for criminological theories, is the most substantial and sophisticated criminological engagement with narrative fiction to date. Frauley combines his own work on film with Vincenzo Ruggiero's (2003) work on literature to establish what I call the critical realist framework, which can be characterised in terms of:

(1) language (in literature) or the combination of language and imagery (in cinema) determines the structure of fictional worlds;
(2) the structure of a fictional world determines textual (literary or cinematic) meaning;
(3) the relationship between textual meaning and extratextual reality is determined by the combination of: (a) linguistic (literary) or linguistic and pictorial (cinematic) structure; (b) the analytic languages (discourses) of criminology or sociology; (c) the practices of reading (literature) or viewing (cinema); and (d) the extent to which fiction is characterised by truth as well as invention;
(4) this relationship between representation and reality facilitates the employment of the fictional realities represented in literature and cinema as empirical referents for criminological and sociological theories.

While there is considerable overlap between the critical realist framework and my criminology of narrative fiction, the critical realist framework as it has been employed to date has been restricted to exploring the pedagogic role of narrative fiction, to facilitating, augmenting, or enhancing the communication of knowledge of crime and its control. Frauley's discussion of film as an analytic tool for criminology gestures towards the aetiological value of narrative fiction, the extent to which it provides knowledge of the causes of crime or social harm, but his conception of fictional reality as an empirical referent is in virtue of protracted illustration, that is as an extension of the use of film as an accessible example or instantiation of theory or practice. In consequence, the analytic values of narrative fiction established by Frauley (and Ruggiero) are part and parcel of the pedagogic rather than the aetiological value of narrative fiction. The primary concern of my criminology of narrative fiction is the aetiological value of exemplary narratives and despite the degree of overlap with the critical realist framework, the distinction between the pedagogic and the aetiological roles of narrative fiction in criminology is sufficient to distinguish my theory from Frauley's framework. My criminology of narrative fiction can be conceived as employing a narrative criminological framework to solve the critical realist framework's problem of the aetiological value of narrative fiction. My argument for the aetiological value of exemplary narratives is based on the combination of the three distinct types of value: phenomenological, counterfactual, and mimetic.

Phenomenological criminology

Phenomenological knowledge is knowledge of what a particular lived experience is like. This is sometimes abbreviated as knowledge–what (something is like) and contrasted with both knowledge–that (such and such is so) and knowledge–how (to perform some act). The *phenomenological value* of an exemplary narrative is the extent to which the narrative representation provides knowledge of the lived experience of perpetrating crime or social harm. I demonstrated that narrative fictions can be valuable to criminology in this way in Chapter 4, using two case studies: Martin Amis' (2014) novel, *The Zone of Interest*, and Tom King and Mitch Gerads' (2018) graphic novel, *The Sheriff of Baghdad*.

Amis (2014) employs three literary devices to provide phenomenological knowledge of collaboration in the Nazi genocide of Jews, Jehovah's Witnesses, Roma, Eastern Europeans, the disabled, homosexuals, and socialists in 1939–45. The first of these is the combination of narrators (the three protagonists) and narration (in the first person), which provides direct access to the thoughts of the three perpetrators. Second, the three narrators are compared and contrasted in terms of their motivation for participating in the genocide, examining a range of selfish causes of collaboration. Third, Amis exploits the referential relation between representation and reality to suggest parallels between the concentration, extermination, and labour camps of Auschwitz and the detention camp in Guantanamo Bay.

King and Gerads (2018) employ three literary and graphic devices in *The Sheriff of Babylon* to provide phenomenological knowledge of collaboration in the mass harm of the Coalition Forces occupation of Iraq. First, the juxtapositioning of the three protagonists – an American contractor, a Sunni expatriate, and a Shia police chief – whose interests diverge and intersect on multiple occasions as the narrative progresses. Second, Gerads provides an immersive representation of the sights and sounds of the hyper-violent environment in which the American protagonist, with whom I was primarily concerned, finds himself. Third, the subversion of the expectations created by the murder mystery genre in order to reveal occupied Baghdad as an epistemic and moral vacuum in which the consequences of actions cannot be predicted and in which meaning is arbitrary.

In each of the case studies, the combination of literary and/or graphic devices provides knowledge of the lived experience of perpetrating, collaborating in, or facilitating social harm. This phenomenological knowledge constitutes the phenomenological value of *The Zone of Interest* and *The Sheriff of Babylon* respectively and this phenomenological value is part and parcel of the works' respective criminological values in virtue of its aetiological character. I concluded that in providing phenomenological knowledge of the lived experience of the fictional offenders, the case studies provide explanations of the causes of actual social harm, data that could be employed in the reduction or prevention of those social harms.

Counterfactual criminology

Counterfactual knowledge is knowledge of reality that is provided by the exploration of alternatives to that reality. Exemplary narratives explore alternative realities in at least two different ways. *Ideal counterfactuals* pair a particular set of circumstances with a preferred response to those circumstances and the relationship between representation and reality is such that the knowledge provided for the fictional world holds for any actual world (past, present, or future) in which the ideal occurs. *Probable counterfactuals* simultaneously represent an alternative to reality and suggest that this alternative may be partially or totally true, that the fictional explanation of circumstances, practices, or theory may be the actual historical or contemporary explanation. The *counterfactual value* of an exemplary narrative is the extent to which the narrative representation provides knowledge of reality by means of exploring alternatives to that reality. I demonstrated that narrative fictions can be valuable to criminology in this way in Chapter 5, using two case studies: ITV's *Broadchurch 3* (2017) television series and Marlon James' (2014) novel, *A Brief History of Seven Killings*.

Broadchurch 3 is an example of an ideal counterfactual and provides knowledge of the legal and moral responsibility for rape by means of the integration of narrative content with narrative form, specifically the combination of changes in the circumstances of the rape represented in the narrative with changes in the framework from which the victim is viewed. The studio creates a cinematic experience in which the audience is encouraged to accept one or more rape myths as the season progresses before revealing those myths and the victim blaming with which they are associated as unambiguously irresponsible and unethical.

A Brief History of Seven Killings is an example of a probable counterfactual, providing knowledge of the causes of organised crime in Jamaica and New York in the last quarter of the twentieth century in particular as well as the role of international politics in crime causation in general. This knowledge is provided by blurring the distinction between representation and reality at two levels, the novel's subject (which is about both the rise and fall of a fictional gangster and the likelihood of actual CIA involvement in Jamaican politics during the Cold War) and the novel's characters, settings, and action (some of which are real, some of which are fictionalised versions of reality, and some of which are fictional).

In the case studies, cinematic and literary devices are employed to provide counterfactual knowledge of causes of crime by means of exploring alternatives to reality or, more accurately, by means of exploring the alternative reality of a narrative fiction. The counterfactual knowledge constitutes the counterfactual value of *Broadchurch 3* and *A Brief History of Seven Killings* respectively and this counterfactual value is part and parcel of the works' respective criminological values in virtue of its aetiological character. I concluded that in providing counterfactual knowledge of the appeal of rape myths and the role of international politics in crime, the case studies provide explanations of the causes of actual crime, data that could be employed in the reduction or prevention of those crimes.

Mimetic criminology

Mimetic knowledge is knowledge of everyday reality that is detailed and accurate. The *mimetic value* of an exemplary narrative is the extent to which the narrative representation provides knowledge of the world by representing everyday reality in detail and with accuracy. Although exemplary narratives across different modes of representation can provide mimetic knowledge, there is a particularly robust relationship between the cinematic mode of representation and mimetic value as a result of the characteristic realism of the cinematic mode of representation, which is the extent to which cinematic narratives appear to reproduce rather than represent reality. I demonstrated that narrative fictions can be valuable to criminology in this way in Chapter 6, using two case studies: Michael Mann's *Miami Vice* (2006) and Fernando Meirelles and Kátia Lund's *City of God* (2002).

In *Miami Vice*, Mann employs stylistic and structural devices to provide detailed and accurate knowledge of the absolute power wielded by the senior management of organised criminal enterprises. I analysed the way in which this knowledge is provided by means of an analysis of a particular scene in the film, in which the two protagonists are interviewed by the apparent head of a South American cocaine cartel. My analysis included a discussion of the relevance of the place of the scene within the overall narrative, which demonstrated how narrative fictions (cinematic and other) create layers of implicit meaning in addition to the explicit information conveyed.

In *City of God*, Meirelles and Lund employ self-reflexive storytelling and a complicated narrative architecture to provide detailed and accurate knowledge of the motivations for collaboration and cooperation with, and resistance to, organised criminal enterprises in deprived communities. I showed how the self-reflexive narration and narrative architecture reproduced the way in which the multiple motivations of the characters overlapped, intersected, and opposed one another to create a situation that impeded resistance to organised criminal enterprises. I also noted that there were various other ways in which the exemplary narrative could be considered as paradigmatic in providing mimetic knowledge, including: being a fictionalised autobiography, the employment of amateur actors who were encouraged to improvise, and the use of an actual *conjunto* for the filming location.

In each of the case studies, stylistic and narrative devices are employed to provide detailed and accurate knowledge of organised criminal enterprises, specifically the absolute power wielded by senior management and the obstacles to resisting organised crime. This mimetic knowledge constitutes the mimetic value of *Miami Vice* and *City of God* and the mimetic value is part and parcel of the works' respective criminological value in virtue of its aetiological character. I concluded that in providing mimetic knowledge of the power and acceptance of organised crime, the case studies provide explanations of the causes of actual crime, data that could be employed in the reduction or prevention of those crimes.

Criminological cinema

In combining the phenomenological, counterfactual, and mimetic values of exemplary narratives, my argument moves beyond the previous criminological engagements with fiction to demonstrate the aetiological role of fiction, fiction as a source of data about the causes of crime and social harm. Although my criminology of narrative fiction is primarily concerned with establishing this aetiological value – which, in turn, constitutes the primary contribution of my theory to the discipline of criminology – I have no desire to minimise the significance of the pedagogic value of exemplary narratives. In consequence, I focused on pedagogic value in Chapter 7, the purpose of which was to explain the relationship between pedagogic and aetiological value within my criminology of narrative fiction. My focus was exclusively on *criminological cinema* – Hollywood feature films that take crime or social harm or the control of crime or social harm as their subject – on the basis of the relevance of audience size to pedagogic value. Simply stated, the larger the audience an exemplary narrative reaches, the greater the facilitation of the communication of knowledge. I began by describing pedagogic value as a function of accessible communication and audience engagement and proposed that the characteristic realism of the cinematic mode of representation and the mythic storytelling characteristic of the Hollywood film industry contributed to both accessible communication and audience engagement. The characteristic realism of the cinematic mode of representation facilitates accessible communication because cinematic representations typically require minimal interpretation and are usually more accessible – more easily and more quickly understood – than hybrid or literary representations. Unlike literary and hybrid representations, feature films engage audiences on two sensory levels, visual and audial, such that the experience of watching a film is more immersive than that of reading a novel or graphic novel. Similarly, there is something about the mythic mode of storytelling that enhances audience engagement, as evinced by the combination of audience participation and repeat viewings. The mode of storytelling also contributes to accessible communication, however, because the structure it employs is one with which all audiences are familiar, from their earliest memories of listening to stories. With regard to narrative form, we know what to expect when we watch a Hollywood feature film, which makes it easier to follow the narrative content represented. The combination of the characteristic realism of the cinematic mode of representation and the mythic mode of storytelling in Hollywood feature films thus contributes to the accessible communication and the audience engagement that constitute the pedagogic value of criminological cinema.

I used Martin Brest's *Beverly Hills Cop* (1984) as a case study of pedagogic value, selected for its popularity within the crime film genre, which suggests that it has been watched by an audience of hundreds of millions of people across the globe over the last three and a half decades. The feature film serves as a particularly good example of the pedagogic potential of criminological cinema because it facilitates the communication of knowledge (about intersectionality) in spite of Brest's decision to sacrifice criminological and sociological content (the representation of racism) to commercial interests. I concluded that the pedagogic value of exemplary narratives is complementary to the aetiological value of exemplary narratives in my criminology of narrative fiction.

Videogame narratives?

Having summarised the steps by which I constructed my criminology of narrative fiction, I address what appears to be a glaring omission in the theory. In his commentary on *Narrative Justice* (McGregor 2018b), Vladimir Rizov (2020) applies the approach I take to narrative representation – including my conceptions of exemplary narratives, the standard mode of engagement, and emplotment – to analyse a questline called *The Iniquities of History* in the videogame *Red Dead Redemption 2* (Rockstar Studios 2018). Rizov's explicit critique of my position concerns the philosophical tradition with which I engage, but his implicit critique applies to both my theory of narrative justice and my criminology of narrative fiction, that they omit videogame narratives from their respective analyses of narrative representation. My criminology of narrative fiction is based on the aetiological value of exemplary narratives and their aetiological value is constituted by the combination of their phenomenological, counterfactual, and mimetic values. These values are in turn constituted by the provision of the three respective types of knowledge, which are gained by the readers or audience who adopt the standard mode of engagement to the exemplary narrative. Crucial to the conveyance of this knowledge from the author or director to the reader or audience by means of the exemplary narrative is the *experience* of that representation. The representation must not only be experienced, but experienced in a particular way (or in one of several ways), determined by the narrative framework. As Rizov points out, *Red Dead Redemption 2* is not just a narrative fiction, but an exemplary one with a narrative framework and a standard mode of engagement. The mimetic knowledge *The Inequities of History* provides about slavery and the mimetic knowledge *The Departed* provides about undercover policing are similarly both provided by the audio-visual experience of a cinematic fiction. Given that phenomenological knowledge is knowledge of what a particular lived experience is like, one might think that that the experience of playing *Red Dead Redemption 2* has the potential for greater phenomenological value than the experience of watching *The Departed* – in virtue of the videogame's essential interactivity.

Aaron Smuts (2009) argues that there is no necessary relation between either internet technology or digital media on the one hand and interactivity on the other. After examining five popular but unsatisfactory accounts of the concept, he defines interactivity as a type of responsiveness that sits between the controllable (completely determined responses) and the random (completely unpredictable responses) and is, in consequence, characteristically mutual. Interactivity thus conceived ranges between maximal, when it cannot be mastered at all, and minimal, when it can be mastered with ease. Smuts explains interactivity in terms of philosopher R.G. Collingwood's (1938) conception of *concreativity*, which describes works of art where the audience exercises some control in structuring their own experience. My interest is, as I have emphasised throughout this book, is in the conventions of representation rather than the practice of art, but Collingwood's claim also holds for performed representations. In a theatrical representation (but not a cinematic one) actors can respond to the reactions of the audience. One might thus consider theatrical representation as maximally interactive and a videogame representation as minimally interactive. Bearing Smuts' initial argument in mind, however, it is important to remember that it is the *game* in 'videogame' that makes it interactive rather than the *video*. Gamebooks, such as Edward Packard's (1979) *Choose Your Own Adventure* and Joe Dever's (1984) *Lone Wolf* series, were very popular in the nineteen eighties and are minimally interactive in the same way as videogames, employing the literary mode of representation. In an earlier paper on the artistic status of videogames, Smuts (2005) concludes: 'Video games are the first concreative mass art.'[2] Gaut (2010) discusses the various claims that interaction and narration are mutually exclusive and reaches a similar conclusion, that interactive narration is not only a coherent concept, but has artistic value in itself. In other words, neither Smuts nor Gaut recognise a significant difference between non-interactive and interactive works within cinematic art.

I agree with most of what Smuts and Gaut have to say about concreativity and interactive narration respectively, but disagree about the significance of the distinction between interactivity and non-interactivity within a particular mode of representation. Videogames such as *Grand Theft Auto V* (Rockstar North 2013) and *Call of Duty: Modern Warfare* (Infinity Ward 2019) may well provide phenomenological, counterfactual, and mimetic knowledge about crime and social harm – as much or perhaps even more than, for example, *Miami Vice* or *Zero Dark Thirty* – but they provide it in a different way, eliciting a different type of imaginative engagement from audiences. In *Zero Dark Thirty*, the audience retains a distance from the fictional protagonist, Maya, even as audience members sympathise, empathise, identify with, or imitate her. In *Call of Duty: Modern Warfare*, this distance is reduced as the player imagines themselves to be Alex, that is to actually be the fictional character in the fictional world. The latter experience is distinct from the most intense identification with (or imitation of) Maya because the standard mode of engagement to *Zero Dark Thirty* involves neither imagining oneself as being Maya nor imagining the events of the film as happening to oneself. This contrasts with not only first-person but also third-person perspective videogames, where players adopt the persona of a character in the world of the game. There is an egocentricity in the imaginative engagement with interactive representations that is absent in the imaginative engagement with non-interactive representations. In philosophy, there is a long tradition of referring to this absence of egocentricity or *disinterest* as a particular type of attention and of *aesthetic attention* being crucial to the various values associated with the experience of representations, art, and beauty (Hutcheson 1725; Kant 1790; Coleridge 1817; Schopenhauer 1818; Bullough 1957; Nanay 2017). To establish and maintain such a distinction is not, however, to diminish the criminological value of videogames, which seems both potentially rich and largely unexplored. In a similar manner to my suggestion that the exploration of the criminological value of the Indian, Nigerian, and Chinese film industries was better left to those with the relevant expertise in Chapter 7, so the inquiry into the aetiological values of videogames is for someone else to undertake. Whoever its author may be, that is a book I very much look forward to reading.

Notes

Chapter 1
[1] Literally, 'in the midst of things'.
[2] With respect to criminology, the aetiological value of a narrative fiction is the extent to which it provides knowledge of the causes of crime or social harm and the pedagogic value of a narrative fiction the extent to which it facilitates, augments, or enhances the communication of criminological knowledge.

Chapter 2
[1] 'Turn' refers to an informal process in which a particular way of doing research becomes popular within a particular academic discipline and then spreads to other disciplines, sometimes even crossing the division between the humanities and the sciences. The structural turn in literary criticism involved approaching texts as self-contained realities and the linguistic turn in the humanities involved a focus on the significance of language. Formalism is a theory of art (including literature) that locates the artistic value of a work of art exclusively in its form (rather than in its content or in a combination of the two).
[2] Historiography is the study of the way in which history is represented by historians and is sometimes referred to as 'the history of history'.
[3] The uroboros is a circular symbol that depicts a snake eating its own tail and is associated with the concept of cyclic renewal.
[4] A hypothesis is a prediction of the links among explanatory factors in research.
[5] 'Substantive' as used here is synonymous with 'content-based'.
[6] See: Baudrillard (1981).
[7] '*Mise-en-scène*' refers to the appearance and arrangement of all the elements that constitute a camera shot.
[8] 'Figurativeness' as used here is synonymous with 'tropes': all literary or rhetorical devices that use words in other than their literal sense.

Chapter 3
[1] I served as a senior constable in the Durban City Police, a South African police service that also no longer exists, 1992–98.
[2] The study was completed in 2016 and is titled, 'A Case Study of a Case Study: Using Ridley Scott's *Black Hawk Down* to Teach Command and Control'.
[3] I have no doubt that narrative justice is a valid criminological methodology, but I do have concerns as to its reliability – at the inter-researcher rather than intra-researcher level (Perri 6 and Bellamy 2011). I discuss other problems with narrative justice as narrative criminology in my conclusion to the *Journal of Aesthetic Education* symposium (McGregor 2020b).

Chapter 4
[1] Teresa Mendoza is the protagonist of *Queen of the South* (2016–19) and is played by Alice Braga.

[2]   *The Zone of Interest* is Amis' second novel about the Nazi genocide. The first, *Time's Arrow: or The Nature of the Offence* (Amis 1991), is also valuable from a criminological perspective.

Chapter 5

[1]   In the UK, series is often used to refer to both a particular series (for example, *Broadchurch 3*) and the series as a whole (for example, *Broadchurch 1–3*). In order to avoid confusion, I employ the American convention of series to refer to the whole and season to refer to its constituent parts.

Chapter 6

[1]   I have used the scene in which Moss is ambushed as an example of both sympathy and empathy and either response would be consistent with the standard mode of engagement to *No Country for Old Men*. The example also serves as a reminder that one can empathise in the absence of mimicry (mimicry is not a necessary condition for empathy).

Chapter 7

[1]   For a well-informed and incisive overview and evaluation of ultra-realism as a criminological framework, see: Wood (2019).

[2]   *Criminology Goes to the Movies* (Rafter and Brown 2011) is an excellent key text for first year introductory modules (such as 'Introduction to Criminology' and 'Introduction to Criminological Theory' in my previous and current institutions) and could easily be used as a scheme of learning for the entire module.

[3]   I made extensive use of *Jaws* (1975) in my creative writing pedagogic practice 2016–18.

Chapter 8

[1]   If this kind of conversation seems unlikely in a police briefing, it would certainly not have been out of place during my own police service (see: Chapter 3, note 1).

[2]   Given my comments on gamebooks, I think Smuts makes two errors in this short sentence: first, there is a significant difference between the creative and concreative categories of representation; and second, even if videogames are concreative art, they were not the first of their kind.

References

13th (2016). Directed by Ava DuVernay. US: Netflix.

Abbott, M. and Gaylin, A. (2018). *Normandy Gold*. London: Titan Comics.

Adorno, T.W. (1966/1973). *Negative Dialectics*. Trans. E.B. Ashton. New York: Continuum.

Agnew, R. (2011). *Toward a Unified Criminology: Integrating Assumptions about Crime, People, and Society*. New York: New York University Press.

Akrivos, D. and Antoniou, A.K. (2019). Conclusion: Popular Criminology Revisited. In: Akrivos, D. and Antoniou, A.K. (eds.). *Crime, Deviance and Popular Culture*. London: Palgrave Macmillan, 335–38.

Amis, M. (1991). *Time's Arrow: or The Nature of the Offence*. London: Jonathan Cape.

Amis, M. (2014). *The Zone of Interest*. London: Jonathan Cape.

Antonopoulos, G.A. and Papanicolaou, G. (2018). *Organized Crime: A Very Short Introduction*. Oxford: Oxford University Press.

Aristotle. (2004). *Poetics*. Trans. P. Murray and T.S. Dorsch. In: Murray, P. (ed.). *Classical Literary Criticism*. London: Penguin, 57–97.

Arnold, R. (1990). Processes of Victimization and Criminalization of Black Women. *Social Justice*, 17 (3), 153–66.

Atkinson, R. and Beer, D. (2010). The Ivorine Tower in the City: Engaging Urban Studies after The Wire. *City*, 14 (5), 529–44.

Attridge, D. (2015). *The Work of Literature*. Oxford: Oxford University Press.

Associated Press (2013). Guantanamo Detainees' Hunger Strikes will no Longer be Disclosed by U.S. Military. *The Washington Post*. 4 December. Available at: www.washingtonpost.com/world/national-security/guantanamo-detainees-hunger-strikes-will-no-longer-be-disclosed-by-us-military/2013/12/04/f6b1aa96-5d24-11e3-bc56-c6ca94801fac_story.html?noredirect=on&utm_term=.e15aefb835e6

Baldwin, J. (1964). *Blues for Mister Charlie*. New York: Dial Press.

Baldwin, T.W. (1947). *Shakspere's Five-Act Structure: Shakspere's Early Plays on the Background of Renaissance Theories of Five-Act Structure from 1470*. Urbana, IL: University of Illinois Press.

Baudrillard, J. (1981/1994). *Simulacra and Simulation*. Trans. S.F. Glaser. Ann Arbor, MI: University of Michigan Press.

Bazin, A. (1958/1967). *What is Cinema? Volume I*. Trans. H. Gray. Los Angeles: University of California Press.

Beauchamp, S. (2016). The Best Retelling of the Iraq War Story Is a Comic Book. *Vulture*, Sequential Art. 4 August. Available at: www.vulture.com/2016/07/sheriff-of-babylon-comic-book-iraq-war.html

Becker, H.S. (1966). Introduction. In: Shaw, C.R. *The Jack-Roller: A Delinquent Boy's Own Story*. Chicago: University of Chicago Press, v–xviii.

Bell, C. (1913). *Art*. New York: Frederick A. Stokes.

Belsey, C. (2011). *A Future for Criticism*. Malden, MA: Wiley-Blackwell.

Benjamin, W. (1933a/2005). Doctrine of the Similar. In: Benjamin, W. *Walter Benjamin: Selected Writings, Volume 2: Part 2 1931–1934*. Trans. R. Livingstone. Cambridge, MA: Harvard University Press, 694–711.

Benjamin, W. (1933b/2005). On the Mimetic Faculty. In: Benjamin, W. *Walter Benjamin: Selected Writings, Volume 2: Part 2 1931–1934*. Trans. R. Livingstone. Cambridge, MA: Harvard University Press, 720–27.

Benney, M. and Hughes, E.C. (1956). Of Sociology and the Interview: Editorial Preface. *The American Journal of Sociology*, LXII (2), 137–42.

Beverly Hills Cop (1984). Directed by Martin Brest. US: Paramount Pictures.

Beverly Hills Cop II (1987). Directed by Tony Scott. US: Paramount Pictures.

Beverly Hills Cop III (1994). Directed by John Landis. US: Paramount Pictures.

Bhaskar, R. (1975). *A Realist Theory of Science*. London: Verso.

Bhaskar, R. (1987). *Scientific Realism and Human Emancipation*. London: Verso.

Bhaskar, R. (1989). *Reclaiming Reality: A Critical Introduction to Contemporary Philosophy*. London: Verso.

Bilton, M. (2006). *Wicked Beyond Belief: The Hunt for the Yorkshire Ripper*. Rev. ed. London: Harper Perennial.

Blaque, K. (2019). *What Is: Intersectionality*. YouTube. 9 January. Available at: www.youtube.com/watch?v=lEeP_3vmdBY

Bleek, W.H.I. (1869). *On the Origin of Language*. Trans. T. Davidson. New York: L.W. Schmidt.

Bordwell, D., Thompson, K. and Smith, J. (2017). *Film-Art: An Introduction*. 11th ed. New York: McGraw-Hill Education.

Boukli, A. and Kotzé, J. (eds.) (2018). *Zemiology: Reconnecting Crime and Social Harm*. London: Palgrave Macmillan.

Bourdieu, P. (1979/1984). *Distinction: A Social Critique of the Judgment of Taste*. Trans. R. Nice. Cambridge, MA: Harvard University Press.

Bourdieu, P. (1980/1990). *The Logic of Practice*. Cambridge: Polity Press.

Bray, C. (2007). The Blair Snitch Project: Thriller Pulps Britain's Ex-Prime Minister. *New York Observer*. 13 November. Available at: https://observer.com/2007/11/the-blair-snitch-project-thriller-pulps-britains-exprime-minister

Breaking Bad (2008–13). Originally released 20 January. US: AMC.

Brisman, A. (2016). On Narrative and Green Cultural Criminology. *International Journal for Crime, Justice and Social Democracy*, 6 (2), 64–77.

Brisman, A. (2019). The Fable of *The Three Little Pigs*: Climate Change and Green Cultural Criminology. *International Journal for Crime, Justice and Social Democracy*, 8 (1), 46–69.

British Film Institute (2019). *Film at the Cinema*. 25 July. Available at: www.bfi.org.uk/sites/bfi.org.uk/files/downloads/bfi-film-at-the-cinema-2019-07-25.pdf

Broadchurch (2013–17). Originally released 4 March. UK: ITV.

Broadchurch (series 1) (2013). Originally released 4 March. UK: ITV.

Broadchurch (series 2) (2015). Originally released 15 January. UK: ITV.

Broadchurch (series 3) (2017). Originally released 27 February. UK: ITV.

Brooks, P. (1984/1992). *Reading for the Plot: Design and Intention in Narrative*. Cambridge, MA: Harvard University Press.

Brown, M. (2004). Crime Fiction and Criminology. *Criminal Justice Review*, 29 (1), 206–20.

Brownmiller, S. (1975). *Against Our Will: Men, Women and Rape*. New York: Simon & Schuster.

Bullough, E. (1957). *Aesthetics: Lectures and Essays*. London: Bowes & Bowes.

Bunker, E. (1977). *The Animal Factory*. New York: Viking Press.

Bunker, E. (1981). *Little Boy Blue*. New York: St Martin's Griffin.

Burgess, E.W. (1930/1966). Discussion. In: Shaw, C.R. *The Jack-Roller: A Delinquent Boy's Own Story*. Chicago: University of Chicago Press, 185–97.

Bureau of the Census (1984). *Statistical Abstract of the United States: 1985 (105th edition)*. Washington, DC. Available at: www.census.gov/library/publications/1984/compendia/statab/105ed.html

Burri, A. (2007/2009). Art and the View from Nowhere. In: Gibson, J., Huerner, W. and Pocci, L (eds). *A Sense of the World: Essays on Fiction, Narrative, and Knowledge*. London: Routledge, 308–17.

Byford, L. (1981). *The Yorkshire Ripper Case: Review of the Police Investigation of the Case by Lawrence Byford, Esq., CBE., QPM., Her Majesty's Inspectorate of Constabulary*. Home Office, December. Available at: https://webarchive.nationalarchives.gov.uk/20090121213042/http://www.homeoffice.gov.uk/about-us/freedom-of-information/released-information/foi-archive-crime/1941-Byford-report/

Canter, D. (1994). *Criminal Shadows: Inside the Mind of a Serial Killer*. London: Harper Collins.

Campbell, J. (1949/2008). *The Hero with a Thousand Faces*. Novato, CA: New World Library.

Capote, T. (1966). *In Cold Blood: A True Account of a Multiple Murder and Its Consequences*. New York: Random House.

Carroll, N. (2001). *Beyond Aesthetics: Philosophical Essays*. New York: Cambridge University Press.

Carroll, N. (2013). *Minerva's Night Out: Philosophy, Pop Culture, and Moving Pictures*. Malden, MA: Wiley-Blackwell.

Casino (1995). Directed by Martin Scorsese. US: Universal Pictures.

Cavender, G. (2004). Media and Crime Policy: A Reconsideration of David Garland's *The Culture of Control*. *Punishment & Society*, 6 (3), 335–48.

Cavender, J. and Jurik, N.C. (2012). *Justice Provocateur: Jane Tennison and Policing in* Prime Suspect. Champaign, IL: Illinois University Press.

Chilcot, J. (2016). *The Report of the Iraq Inquiry*. 6 July. Available at: https://webarchive.nationalarchives.gov.uk/20171123122743/http://www.iraqinquiry.org.uk/the-report/

City of God [*Cidade de Deus*] (2002). Directed by Fernando Meirelles and Kátia Lund. Brazil: Miramax Films.

Cohen, A. (1955). *Delinquent Boys: The Culture of the Gang*. New York: Free Press.

Coleridge, S.T. (1817/1949). *Biographia Literaria and Aesthetical Essays*. Oxford: Oxford University Press.

College of Policing (2019). *Equality Impact Analysis: Implementation of the new entry routes for police constables. Version 1.0*. May. Available at: www.college.police.uk/What-we-do/Learning/Policing-Education-Qualifications-Framework/Entry-routes-for-police-constables/Documents/Equality-Impact-Analysis-Implementation-of-new%20entry-routes-for-police-constables.pdf

Collingwood, R.G. (1938). *The Principles of Art*. New York: Oxford University Press.

Combahee River Collective (1977). *The Combahee River Collective Statement*. Available at: https://combaheerivercollective.weebly.com/the-combahee-river-collective-statement.html

Conetta, C. (2003). *The Wages of War: Iraqi Combatant and Noncombatant Fatalities in the 2003 Conflict*. Project on Defense Alternatives. *Research Monograph* 8. 20 October. Available at: www.comw.org/pda/0310rm8.html

Conrad, P. and Schneider, J. (1980). *Deviance and Medicalization: From Badness to Sickness*. St Louis, MO: Mosby.

Conwell, C. and Sutherland, E.H. (1937). *The Professional Thief*. Chicago, IL: University of Chicago Press.

Coomber, R., Moyle, L. and Mahoney, M.K. (2019). Symbolic Policing: Situating Targeted Police Operations/'Crackdowns' on Street-Level Drug Markets. *Policing and Society*, 29 (1), 1–17.

Cop Land (1997). Directed by James Mangold. US: Miramax Films.

Crenshaw, K.W. (1989). Demarginalizing the Intersection of Race and Sex: A Black Feminist Critique of Antidiscrimination Doctrine, Feminist Theory and Antiracist Politics. *University of Chicago Legal Forum*, 1989 (1), 139–67.

Currie, G. (1995). *Image and Mind: Film, Philosophy, and Cognitive Science*. Cambridge: Cambridge University Press.

Currie, G. (2010). *Narratives & Narrators: A Philosophy of Stories*. Oxford: Oxford University Press.

Dallaire, R. (2003). *Shake Hands with the Devil: The Failure of Humanity in Rwanda*. London: Arrow.

Darwin, C.R. (1871). *The Descent of Man, and Selection in Relation to Sex*, Volume I. London: John Murray.

Deleuze, G. (1983/2005). *Cinema I: The Movement-Image*. Trans. H. Tomlinson and B. Habberjam. London: Continuum.

Deleuze, G. (1985/2013). *Cinema II: The Time-Image*. Trans. H. Tomlinson. London: Bloomsbury.

Dever, J. (1984). *Lone Wolf Book 1: Flight from the Dark*. London: Sparrow Books.

Dick, P.K. (1962). *The Man in the High Castle*. New York: Putnam.

Diken, B. and Laustsen, C.B. (2007). *Sociology through the Projector*. Abingdon: Routledge.

Donnie Brasco (1997). Directed by Mike Newell. US: TriStar Pictures.

Dorhn, D. (2009). Counterfactual Narrative Explanation. *The Journal of Aesthetics and Art Criticism*, 67 (1), 37–47.

Drake, St C. and Cayton, H.R. (1945/1993). *Black Metropolis: A Study of Negro Life in a Northern City*. Chicago: Chicago University Press.

Dulles, J.W.F. (1996). *Carlos Austin, Brazilian Crusader Volume II: The Years 1960–1977*. Austin, TX: University of Texas Press.

Elliott, J. (2005). *Using Narrative in Social Research: Qualitative and Quantitative Approaches*. London: SAGE Publications.

Ellroy, J. (1995). *American Tabloid*. London: Arrow.

Ellroy, J. (2001). *The Cold Six Thousand*. London: Windmill.

Ellroy, J. (2009). *Blood's a Rover*. London: Windmill.

End of Watch (2012). Directed by David Ayer. US: Open Road Films.

E.T. the Extra-Terrestrial (1982). Directed by Steven Spielberg. US: Universal Pictures.

Falling Down (1993). Directed by Joel Schumacher. US: Warner Bros.

Farber, D. (2019). *Crack: Rock Cocaine, Street Capitalism, and the Decade of Greed*. New York: Cambridge University Press.

Fear the Walking Dead (2015–19). Originally released 23 August. US: AMC.

Ferrell, J. (1995). Culture, Crime, and Cultural Criminology. *Journal of Criminal Justice and Popular Culture*, 3 (2), 25–42.

Ferrell, J. (1996). *Crimes of Style: Urban Graffiti and the Politics of Criminality*. Boston, MA: Northeastern.

Ferrell, J. (1999). Cultural Criminology. *Annual Review of Sociology*, 25, 395–418.

Ferrell, J., Hayward, K. and Young, J. (2015). *Cultural Criminology: An Invitation*. 2nd ed. London: SAGE Publications.

Fleetwood, J. (2014). *Drug Mules: Women in the International Cocaine Trade*. Basingstoke: Palgrave Macmillan.

Fleetwood, J., Presser, L., Sandberg, S. and Ugelvik, T. (eds) (2019). *The Emerald Handbook of Narrative Criminology*. Bingley: Emerald Publishing Limited.

Foucault, M. (1961/2006). *Madness and Civilization: A History of Insanity in the Age of Reason*. Trans. J. Murphy and J. Khalfa. New York: Routledge.

Foucault, M. (1975/1977). *Discipline and Punish: The Birth of the Prison*. Trans. A. Sheridan. New York: Pantheon Books.

Foucault, M. (1976/1978). *The History of Sexuality Volume 1: The Will to Knowledge*. Trans. R. Hurley. New York: Random House.

Frauley, J. (2010). *Criminology, Deviance, and the Silver Screen: The Fictional Reality and the Criminological Imagination*. New York: Palgrave Macmillan.

Freytag, G. (1894/1900). *Freytag's Technique of the Drama, An Exposition of Dramatic Composition and Art by Dr. Gustav Freytag: An Authorized Translation from the Sixth German Edition*. Trans. E.J. MacEwan. Chicago, IL: Scott, Foresman & Company.

Gane-McCalla, C. (2016). *Inside the CIA's Secret War in America*. Los Angeles, CA: Over the Edge Books.

Garland, D. (2001). *The Culture of Control: Crime and Social Order in Contemporary Society*. Oxford: Oxford University Press.

Gaut, B. (2010). *A Philosophy of Cinematic Art*. Cambridge: Cambridge University Press.

Genette, G. (1972/1980). *Narrative Discourse: An Essay in Method*. Trans. J.E. Lewin. Ithaca, NY: Cornell University Press.

Gibson, J. (2007). *Fiction and the Weave of Life*. Oxford: Oxford University Press.

Gibson, J. (2008). Cognitivism and the Arts. *Philosophy Compass*, 3 (4), 573–89.

Girard, R. (1978/1987). *Things Hidden since the Foundation of the World*. Trans. S. Bann and M. Metteer. London: The Athlone Press.

Goldie, P. (2012). *The Mess Inside: Narrative, Emotion, and the Mind*. Oxford: Oxford University Press.

Gombrich, E.H. (1950). *The Story of Art*. London: Phaidon Press.

Goodfellas (1990). Directed by Martin Scorsese. US: Warner Bros.

Grim, R., Sledge, M. and Ferner, M. (2014). Key Figures in CIA-Crack Cocaine Scandal Begin to Come Forward. *HuffPost US*. 10 October. Available at: www.huffingtonpost.co.uk/entry/gary-webb-dark-lliance_n_5961748

Grubb, A. and Turner, E. (2012). Attribution of Blame in Rape Cases: A Review of the Impact of Rape Myth Acceptance, Gender Role Conformity and Substance Use on Victim Blaming. *Aggression and Violent Behavior*, 17 (5), 443–52.

Hall, S. (2012). *Theorizing Crime and Deviance: A New Perspective*. London: SAGE Publications.

Hall, S., Critcher, C., Jefferson, T., Clarke, J. and Roberts, B. (1978). *Policing the Crisis: Mugging, the State, and Law and Order*. London: Macmillan Publishers.

Hall, S., Evans, J. and Nixon, S. (eds) (1997). *Representation*. London: SAGE Publications.

Harfield, C. and Harfield, K. (2018). *Covert Investigation*. 5th ed. Oxford: Oxford University Press.

Harris, R. (1992). *Fatherland*. London: Hutchinson.

Harris, R. (1998). *Archangel*. London: Hutchinson.

Harris, R. (2007). *The Ghost*. London: Hutchinson.

Hayward, K. (2004). *City Limits: Crime, Consumer Culture and the Urban Experience*. London: Glasshouse Press.

Henry, S. and Milovanovic, D. (1996). *Constitutive Criminology: Beyond Postmodernism*. London: SAGE Publications.

Hillyard, P. and Tombs, S. (2004). Beyond Criminology? In: Hillyard, P., Pantazis, C., Tombs, S. and Gordon, D. *Beyond Criminology: Taking Harm Seriously*. London: Pluto Press, 10–29.

Hirschman, D. (2018). Why Sociology Needs Science Fiction. *Contexts*, 17 (3), 13–14.

Hollway, W. and Jefferson, T. (2000). *Doing Qualitative Research Differently: Free Association, Narrative and the Interview Method*. London: SAGE Publications.

Homer (2003). *The Odyssey*. Trans. E.V. Rieu. London: Penguin Books.

Horkheimer, M. and Adorno, T.W. (1947/1989). *Dialectic of Enlightenment*. Trans. J. Cummings. New York: Continuum.

Hutcheson, F. (1725/2008). *An Inquiry into the Original of Our Ideas of Beauty and Virtue*. Indianapolis: Liberty Fund.

Hyvärinen, M. (2010). Revisiting the Narrative Turns. *Life Writing*, 7 (1), 69–82.

Iacoboni, M. (2008). *Mirroring People: The New Science of How We Connect with Others*. New York: Farrar, Strauss & Giroux.

IMBD.com (2019a). *Beverly Hills Cop*. Box Office Mojo. Available at: www.boxofficemojo.com/movies/?id=beverlyhillscop.htm. Accessed 22 July 2019.

IMBD.com (2019b). *Domestic Grosses: Adjusted for Ticket Price Inflation*. Box Office Mojo. Available at: www.boxofficemojo.com/alltime/adjusted.htm?adjust_yr=2018&p=.htm. Accessed 22 July 2019.

Infernal Affairs (2002). Directed by Andrew Lau and Alan Mak. Hong Kong: Media Asian Distribution.

Infinity Ward (2019). *Call of Duty: Modern Warfare*. Santa Monica, CA: Activision.

Iraq Body Count (2019). *Database*. Available at: www.iraqbodycount.org/database/

Irigaray, L. (1977/1985). This Sex Which Is Not One. In: Irigaray, L. *This Sex Which Is Not One*. Trans. C. Porter. New York: Cornell University Press, 23–33.

Jackson, D. (2014). U.S. Sends Five Gitmo Prisoners to Kazakhstan. *USA Today*. 31 December. Available at: https://eu.usatoday.com/story/news/nation/2014/12/31/obama-guantanamo-bay-prison-kazakhstan-transfer/21095095/

James, M. (2014/2015). *A Brief History of Seven Killings*. London: Oneworld Publications.

Jaws (1975). Directed by Steven Spielberg. US: Universal Pictures.

Kahneman, D. and Miller, D.T. (1986). Norm Theory: Comparing Reality to its Alternatives. *Psychological Review*, 93 (2), 136–53.

Kahneman, D. and Tversky, A. (1982). The Simulation Heuristic. In: Kahneman, D., Slovic, P. and Tversky, A. (eds.). *Judgment under Uncertainty: Heuristics and Biases*. New York: Cambridge University Press, 201–208.

Kant, I. (1790/2001). *Critique of the Power of Judgment*. Trans. P. Guyer and E. Matthews. Cambridge: Cambridge University Press.

Katz, J. (1988). *Seductions of Crime: Moral and Sensual Attractions in Doing Evil*. New York: Basic Books.

Käufer, S. and Chemero, A. (2015). *Phenomenology: An Introduction*. Cambridge: Polity Press.

King, T. and Gerads, M. (2016). *Bang. Bang. Bang.* New York: Vertigo Comics.

King, T. and Gerads, M. (2017). *Pow. Pow. Pow.* New York: Vertigo Comics.

King, T. and Gerads, M. (2018). *The Sheriff of Babylon.* Deluxe Edition. Burbank, CA: DC Comics.

Kracauer, S. (1960). *Theory of Film: The Redemption of Physical Reality.* New York: Oxford University Press.

Kruger, R. (1959). *Good-bye Dolly Gray: The Story of the Boer War.* London: Pan.

Labov, W. and Waletzky, J. (1967). Narrative Analysis: Oral Versions of Personal Experience. In: Helm, J. (ed.), *Essays on the Verbal and Visual Arts.* Seattle, WA: University of Washington Press, 12–44.

Lamarque, P. (2009). *The Philosophy of Literature.* Oxford: Blackwell Publishing.

Lamarque, P. (2014). *The Opacity of Narrative.* London: Rowman & Littlefield International.

Lamarque, P. and Olsen, S.H. (1994/2002). *Truth, Fiction, and Literature: A Philosophical Perspective.* Oxford: Clarendon.

Lazar, Z. (2014). 'A Brief History of Seven Killings' by Marlon James. *The New York Times.* 23 October. Available at: www.nytimes.com/2014/10/26/books/review/a-brief-history-of-seven-killings-by-marlon-james-review.html

Lewis, D. (1973). *Counterfactuals.* Oxford: Blackwell.

Lewis, D. (1978). Truth in Fiction. *American Philosophical Quarterly,* 15 (1), 37–46.

Lewis, D. (1983). Truth in Fiction. In: Lewis, D. *Philosophical Papers: Volume 1.* Oxford: Oxford University Press, 261–80.

Lewis, D. (1986). *On the Plurality of Worlds.* Oxford: Blackwell.

Linde, C. (1993). *Life Stories: The Creation of Coherence.* New York: Oxford University Press.

Line of Duty (2012–19). Originally released 26 June. UK: BBC.

Lins, P. (1997/2006). *City of God.* Trans. A. Entrekin. London: Bloomsbury Publishing.

Lyons, J. (2010). *Miami Vice.* Malden, MA: Blackwell.

McAdams, D.P. (1993). *The Stories We Live By: Personal Myths and the Making of the Self.* New York: William Morrow.

McAdams, D.P. (2015/2018). *The Art and Science of Personality Development.* New York: Guildford.

McCarthy, C. (2005). *No Country for Old Men.* New York: Alfred A. Knopf.

McClennen, S.A. (2011). From the Aesthetics of Hunger to the Cosmetics of Hunger in Brazilian Cinema: Meirelles' *City of God*. *symplokē*, 19 (1–2), 95–106.

McGregor, R. (2013). A New/Old Ontology of Film, *Film-Philosophy*, 17 (1), 265–80.

McGregor, R. (2016). *The Value of Literature*. London: Rowman & Littlefield International.

McGregor, R. (2018a). Cinematic Realism: A Defence from Plato to Gaut. *British Journal of Aesthetics*, 58 (3), 225–39.

McGregor, R. (2018b). *Narrative Justice*. London: Rowman & Littlefield International.

McGregor, R. (2019). James Ellroy's Critical Criminology: Crimes of the Powerful in the *Underworld USA Trilogy*, *Critical Criminology: An International Journal*, https://doi.org/10.1007/s10612-019-09459-3

McGregor, R. (2020a). Introduction to the *Narrative Justice* Symposium. *Journal of Aesthetic Education*, 54 (4), 1–5.

McGregor, R. (2020b). Replies to Critics. *Journal of Aesthetic Education*, 54 (4), 62–75.

Manning, P.K. (2010). *Democratic Policing in a Changing World*. Abingdon: Routledge.

Maruna, S. (2001). *Making Good: How Ex-Convicts Reform and Build Their Lives*. Washington, DC: American Psychological Association.

Matravers, D. (2014). *Fiction and Narrative*. Oxford: Oxford University Press.

Marx, K. and Engels, F. (1846/2000). *The German Ideology*. In: Marx, K. *Karl Marx: Selected Writings*. Oxford: Oxford University Press, 175–208.

Matthews, R. (2014). *Realist Criminology*. London: Palgrave Macmillan.

Matza, D. (1964). *Delinquency and Drift*. New York: John Wiley & Sons.

Melville, H. (1851). *Moby-Dick; or, The Whale*. London: Richard Bentley.

Miami Vice (1984–90). Originally released 16 September. US: NBC.

Miami Vice (season 1) (1984). Originally released 16 September. US: NBC.

Miami Vice (2006). Directed by Michael Mann. US: Universal Pictures.

Mills, C.W. (1940). Situated Actions and Vocabularies of Motive. *American Sociological Review*, 5 (6), 904–13.

Mills, C.W. (1959). *The Sociological Imagination*. New York: Oxford University Press.

Mishler, E.G. (1986). *Research Interviewing: Context and Narrative*. Cambridge, MA: Harvard University Press.

Mishler, E.G. (1995). Models of Narrative Analysis: A Typology. *Journal of Narrative and Life History*, 5 (2), 87–123.

Moorcraft, P. and Cohen, M. (1984). *Stander...Bank Robber*. Johannesburg: Galago Publishing.

Motion Picture Association of America (2017). *Theatrical Market Statistics*. March. Available at: www.motionpictures.org/wp-content/uploads/2017/03/MPAA-Theatrical-Market-Statistics-2016_Final.pdf

Murji, K. (1996/2017). Wild Life: Constructions and Representations of Yardies. In: Ferrell, J. and Websdale, N. (eds). *Making Trouble: Cultural Constraints of Crime, Deviance, and Control*. Abingdon: Routledge, 179–202.

Nanay, B. (2017). *Aesthetics as Philosophy of Perception*. Oxford: Oxford University Press.

Nash Information Services, LLC (2019). *Beverly Hills Cop* (1984). The Numbers: Where Data and the Movie Business Meet. Available at: www.the-numbers.com/movie/Beverly-Hills-Cop#tab=summary

National Police Chiefs' Council (2016). *Policing Vision 2025*. 6 November. Available at: www.npcc.police.uk/documents/Policing%20Vision.pdf

No Country for Old Men (2007). Directed by Joel Coen and Ethan Coen. US: Miramax Films.

Packard, E. (1979). *Choose Your Own Adventure 1: The Cave of Time*. New York: Bantam Books.

Page, J. and Goodman, P. (2018). Creative Disruption: Edward Bunker, Carceral Habitus, and the Criminological Value of Fiction. *Theoretical Criminology*, advance access, DOI: https://doi.org/10.1177/1362480618769866

Perito, R.M. (2011). The Iraqi Federal Police: U.S. Police Building Under Fire. United States Institute of Peace, *Special Report 291* (October). Available at: www.usip.org/sites/default/files/resources/SR291_The_Iraq_Federal_Police.pdf

Perlman, J. (2010). *Favela: Four Decades Living on the Edge in Rio de Janeiro*. New York: Oxford University Press.

Perri 6 and Bellamy, C. (2011). *Principles of Methodology: Research Design in Social Science*. London: SAGE Publications.

Plato (1997). *Republic*. Trans. G.M.A. Grube and C.D.C. Reeve. In: Cooper, J.M. (ed.). *Plato: Complete Works*. Indianapolis, IN: Hackett, 971–1223.

Plummer, K. (1994). *Telling Sexual Stories: Power, Change, and Social Worlds*. London: Routledge.

Polkinghorne, Donald E. (1988). *Narrative Knowing and the Human Sciences*. New York: State University of New York Press.

Potter, G. (1998). Truth in Fiction, Science and Criticism. *Journal of Literary Semantics*, 27 (3), 173–89.

Potter, H. (2015). *Intersectionality and Criminology: Disrupting and Revolutionizing Studies of Crime*. London: Routledge.

Presser, L. (2008). *Been a Heavy Life: Stories of Violent Men*. Champaign, IL: University of Illinois Press.

Presser, L. (2009). The Narratives of Offenders. *Theoretical Criminology*, 13 (2), 177–200.

Presser, L. (2013). *Why We Harm*. New Brunswick, NJ: Rutgers University Press.

Presser, L. (2016). Criminology and the Narrative Turn. *Crime, Media, Culture: An International Journal*, 12 (2), 137–51.

Presser, L. (2018). *Inside Story: How Narratives Drive Mass Harm*. Oakland, CA: University of California Press.

Presser, L. and Sandberg, S. (eds) (2015). *Narrative Criminology: Understanding Stories of Crime*. New York: New York University Press.

Presser, L. and Sandberg, S. (eds) (2015a). Introduction. In: Presser, L. and Sandberg, S. (eds). *Narrative Criminology: Understanding Stories of Crime*. New York: New York University Press, 1–20.

Presser, L. and Sandberg, S. (2019). Narrative Criminology as Critical Criminology. *Critical Criminology*, 27 (1), 131–43.

Prime Suspect (1991–2006). Originally released 7 April. UK: ITV.

Queen of the South (2016–19). Originally released 23 June. US: USA Network.

Queen of the South (season 1) (2016). Originally released 23 June 2016. US: USA Network.

Rafter, N. (2006). *Shots in the Mirror: Crime Films and Society*. 2nd ed. New York: Oxford University Press.

Rafter, N. (2007a). *The Departed*. Crime Films: A Monthly Column. 30 January. Available at: https://blog.oup.com/2007/01/the_departed/

Rafter, N. (2007b). Crime, Film and Criminology: Recent Sex-Crime Movies. *Theoretical Criminology*, 11 (3), 403–20.

Rafter, N. and Brown, M. (2011). *Criminology Goes to the Movies: Crime Theory and Popular Culture*. New York: New York University Press.

Rawlings, P. (1992). *Drunks, Whores and Idle Apprentices: Criminal Biographies of the Eighteenth Century*. London: Routledge.

Rawlings, P. (1998). Crime Writers: Non-Fiction Crime Books. *The British Criminology Conferences: Selected Proceedings. Volume 1: Emerging Themes in Criminology*. Available at: www.britsoccrim.org/volume1/010.pdf

Raymen, T. (2018). Living in the End Times through Popular Culture: An Ultra-Realist Analysis of *The Walking Dead* as Popular Criminology. *Crime, Media, Culture: An International Journal*, 14 (3), 429–47.

Raymond, D. (1984). *He Died with His Eyes Open*. London: Secker & Warburg.

Reiner, R. (2019). *The Politics of the Police*. 5th ed. Oxford: Oxford University Press.

Ricks, T.E. (2007). *Fiasco: The American Military Adventure in Iraq*. London: Penguin Books.

Ricoeur, P. (1980). Narrative Time. *Critical Inquiry*, 7 (1), 169–90.

Ricoeur, P. (1983/1984). *Time and Narrative: Volume 1*. Trans. K. McLaughlin and D. Pellauer. Chicago, IL: University of Chicago Press.

Ricoeur, P. (1984/1985). *Time and Narrative: Volume 2*. Trans. K. McLaughlin and D. Pellauer. Chicago, IL: University of Chicago Press.

Ricoeur, P. (1985/1988). *Time and Narrative: Volume 3*. Trans. K. McLaughlin and D. Pellauer. Chicago, IL: University of Chicago Press.

Riessman, C.K. (2002). Analysis of Personal Narratives. In: Gubrium, J.F. and Holstein, J.A. (eds). *Handbook of Interview Research: Context and Method*. Thousand Oaks, CA: SAGE Publications, 695–710.

Rizov, V. (2020). Narrative Redemption: A Commentary on McGregor's *Narrative Justice*. *Journal of Aesthetic Education*, 54 (4), 26–35.

Rockstar North (2013). *Grand Theft Auto V*. PlayStation 3 and Xbox 360. New York: Rockstar Games.

Rockstar Studios (2018). *Red Dead Redemption 2*. PlayStation 4 and Xbox One. New York: Rockstar Games.

Ruggiero, V. (2002). *Moby Dick* and the Crimes of the Economy. *British Journal of Criminology*, 42 (1), 96–108.

Ruggiero, V. (2003). *Crime in Literature: Sociology of Deviance and Fiction*. London: Verso.

Ryle, G. (1949). *The Concept of Mind*. Chicago: University of Chicago Press.

Sandberg, S. (2010). What can "Lies" Tell Us about Life? Notes towards a Framework of Narrative Criminology. *Journal of Criminal Justice Education*, 21 (4), 447–65.

Sandberg, S. and Pedersen, W. (2009). *Street Capital: Black Cannabis Dealers in a White Welfare State*. Bristol: Policy Press.

Sandberg, S. and Ugelvik, T. (2016). The Past, Present, and Future of Narrative Criminology: A Review and an Invitation. *Crime, Media, Culture*, 12 (2), 129–36.

Schiller, J.C.F. (1794/1967). *On the Aesthetic Education of Man: In a Series of Letters*. Trans. E.M. Wilkinson and L.A. Willoughby. London: Oxford University Press.

Schopenhauer, A. (1818/2010). *The World as Will and Representation: Volume I*. Trans. J.N.A. Welchman and C. Janaway. Cambridge: Cambridge University Press.

Schwarz, R. (2001). City of God. *New Left Review*, 12 (Nov–Dec), 102–12.

Seven (1995). Directed by David Fincher. US: New Line Cinema.

Shaw, C.R. (1930/1966). *The Jack-Roller: A Delinquent Boy's Own Story*. Chicago: University of Chicago Press.

Shklovsky. V. (1921/1965). Sterne's *Tristram Shandy*: A Stylistic Commentary. In: Lemon, L.T. and Reis, M.J. (eds). *Russian Formalist Criticism: Four Essays*. Lincoln: University of Nebraska Press, 25–57.

Shone, T. (2004). *Blockbuster: How Hollywood Learned to Stop Worrying and Love the Summer*. London: Simon & Schuster.

Sinnerbrink, R. (2016). *Cinematic Ethics: Exploring Ethical Experience through Film*. Abingdon: Routledge.

Smith, M. (2017). *Film, Art, and the Third Culture: A Naturalized Aesthetics of Film*. Oxford: Oxford University Press.

Smuts, A. (2005). Are Videogames Art? *Contemporary Aesthetics*, 3. Available at: www.contempaesthetics.org/newvolume/pages/article.php?articleID=299

Smuts, A. (2009). What is Interactivity? *Journal of Aesthetic Education*, 43 (4), 53–73.

Spivak, G.C. (2012). *An Aesthetic Education in the Era of Globalization*. Cambridge, MA: Harvard University Press.

Squire, C., Andrews, M. and Tamboukou, M. (2013). Introduction: What is Narrative Research? In: Andrews, M., Squire, C. and Tamboukou, M. (eds). *Doing Narrative Research*. 2nd ed. London: SAGE Publications, 1–26.

Stander (2003). Directed by Bronwen Hughes. South Africa: Newmarket Films.

Star Wars: Episode IV – A New Hope (1977). Directed by George Lucas. US: 20th Century Fox.

Star Wars: Episode V – The Empire Strikes Back (1980). Directed by Irvin Kerschner. US: 20th Century Fox.

Star Wars: Episode VI – Return of the Jedi (1983). Directed by Richard Marquand. US: 20th Century Fox.

Suarez, E. and Gadalla, T.M. (2010). Stop Blaming the Victim: A Meta-Analysis on Rape Myths. *Journal of Interpersonal Violence*, 25 (11), 2010–35.

Sutherland, E.H. (1947). *Principles of Criminology*. 4th ed. Philadelphia, PA: J.B. Lippincott & Co.

Sykes, G.M. and Matza, D. (1957). Techniques of Neutralization: A Theory of Delinquency. *American Sociological Review*, 22 (6), 664–70.

Taussig, M. (1993). *Mimesis and Alterity: A Particular History of the Senses*. New York: Routledge.

Taxi Driver (1976). Directed by Martin Scorsese. US: Columbia Pictures.

Temkin, J., Gray, J.M. and Barrett, J. (2018). Different Functions of Rape Myth Use in Court: Findings From a Trial Observation Study. *Feminist Criminology*, 13 (2), 205–26.

The Departed (2006). Directed by Martin Scorcese. US: Warner Bros.

The Ghost (2010). Directed by Roman Polanski. UK: Optimum Releasing.

The Godfather (1972). Directed by Francis Ford Coppola. US: Paramount Pictures.

The Man in the High Castle (2015–19). Originally released 15 January. US: Amazon Studios.

The Siege (1998). Directed by Edward Zwick. US: 20th Century Fox.

The Walking Dead (2010–19). Originally released 31 October. US: AMC.

The Wire (2002–08). Originally released 2 June. US: HBO.

Thomas, W.I. and Znaniecki, F. (1927). *The Polish Peasant in Europe and America: Volumes I & II*. 2nd ed. New York: Alfred A. Knopf.

Todorov, T. (1971/1977). *The Poetics of Prose*. Trans. R. Howard. Oxford: Blackwell.

Turnbull, S. (2014). *The TV Crime Drama*. Edinburgh: Edinburgh University Press.

Ugelvik, T. (2014). *Power and Resistance in Prison: Doing Time, Doing Freedom*. Basingstoke: Palgrave Macmillan.

Vogler, C. (1992). *The Writer's Journey: Mythic Structure for Storytellers and Screenwriters*. Studio City, CA: Michael Wiese Productions.

Von Lampe, K. (2015). *Organized Crime: Analyzing Illegal Activities, Criminal Structures, and Extra-Legal Governance*. London: Sage.

Wacquant, L. (2000/2004). *Body and Soul: Notebooks of an Apprentice Boxer*. New York: Oxford University Press.

Wacquant, L. (2005). Carnal Connections: On Embodiment, Apprenticeship, and Membership. *Qualitative Sociology*, 28 (4), 445–74.

Wainwright, T. (2016). *Narconomics: How to Run a Drug Cartel*. New York: PublicAffairs.

Wakeman, S. (2018). The 'One Who Knocks' and the 'One Who Waits': Gendered Violence in *Breaking Bad. Crime, Media, Culture: An International Journal*, 14 (2), 213–28.

Walklate, S (2017). *Criminology: The Basics*. 3rd ed. London: Routledge.

Walsh, D. (1969). *Literature and Knowledge*. Middletown, CT: Wesleyan University Press.

Walton, K.L. (1984). Transparent Pictures: On the Nature of Photographic Realism. *Critical Inquiry*, 11 (2), 246–77.

Walton, K.L. (1990). *Mimesis as Make-Believe: On the Foundations of the Representational Arts*. Cambridge, MA: Harvard University Press.

Waltz with Bashir (2008). Directed by Ari Folman. Israel: Sony Pictures Classics.

Webb, G. (1998). *Dark Alliance: The CIA, the Contras, and the Crack Cocaine Explosion*. New York: Seven Stories.

Weiner, T. (2007). *Legacy of Ashes: The History of the CIA*. London: Penguin.

White, H. (1980). The Value of Narrativity in the Representation of Reality. *Critical Inquiry*, 7 (1), 5–27.

White, H. (1987). The Problem of Style in Realistic Representation: Marx and Flaubert. In: Lang, B. (ed.). *The Concept of Style*. Ithaca: Cornell University Press, 279–98.

Wieder, D.L. (1974). *Language and Social Reality: The Case of Telling the Convict Code*. The Hague: Mouton.

Williams, F.P. (1984). The Demise of the Criminological Imagination: A Critique of Recent Criminology. *Justice Quarterly*, 1 (1), 91–106.

Williamson, H. and Keiser, R.L. (1965). *Hustler!* New York: Garden City.

Willis, A. and Sembello, D. (1984). Neutron Dance. New York: RCA Records.

Wilson, C. (1983). Literature and Knowledge. *Philosophy*, 58 (226), 489–96.

Wood, M.A. (2019). What is Realist about Ultra-Realist Criminology? A Critical Appraisal of the Perspective. *Journal of Theoretical and Philosophical Criminology*, 11 (August), 95–114.

Worth, S.E. (2017). *In Defense of Reading*. London: Rowman & Littlefield International.

Wright, R. (1940). *Native Son*. New York: Harper & Brothers.

Wright, R. (1945/1993). Introduction. In: Drake, St C. and Cayton, H.R. *Black Metropolis: A Study of Negro Life in a Northern City*. Chicago, IL: Chicago University Press, xvii–xxxiii.

Yeats, W.B. (1933/2019). Sailing to Byzantium. *Poetry Foundation.* Available at: www.poetryfoundation.org/poems/43291/sailing-to-byzantium

Yorke, J. (2013). *Into the Woods: How Stories Work and Why We Tell Them.* London: Penguin.

Young, J. (2011). *The Criminological Imagination.* Cambridge: Polity Press.

Zero Dark Thirty (2012). Directed by Kathryn Bigelow. US: Sony Pictures Releasing.

Index